PLANTING
FOR
SUN AND SHADE

PLANTING FOR SUN AND SHADE

A superb collection of beautiful flowers for
interest throughout the gardening year

BOB LEGGE • DAVID PAPWORTH
NOËL PROCKTER • MICHAEL UPWARD

 ALAMANDER

SALAMANDER BOOKS LIMITED
129–137 YORK WAY
LONDON N7 9LG
UNITED KINGDOM

A Salamander Book

Published by Salamander Books Ltd.
129–137 York Way
London N7 9LG
United Kingdom

9 8 7 6 5 4 3 2 1

ISBN 0 86101 911 3

All correspondence concerning the content of this book should be addressed to Salamander Books Ltd.

CREDITS

Editor: Dennis Cove
Designer: Paul Johnson
Colour and monochrome
    reproductions: Pixel Tech., Singapore
Filmset: SX Composing DTP, England
Printed In Hong Kong

Photograph captions:
Half-title: Oxalis adenophylla
Title: Tagetes patula
Page 5: Begonia x tuberhybrida
Page 6-7: Hemerocallis

Contents

Preface

Flowers are essential for every garden, offering colour and interest throughout the gardening year. With many thousands of varieties now available, choosing the most appropriate for any particular garden can be difficult. Collected here are a selection of 150 of the very best plants which guarantee a wonderful display for beds and borders in sunny or shaded locations. Many of the gardener's favourites are included and the range covers the complete colour spectrum. Divided into four main sections – annuals, perennials, bulbs and alpines – each part has its own introduction with specialist information on planting, cultivation and propagation to enable every grower to get the most from the available space and sunshine.

Each flower is listed by Latin name and, wherever appropriate, its more common name is given. Every entry provides helpful advice on the types of aspect and soil required for best results, the best growing methods, and effective ways to control pests and diseases. Useful hints highlight special points to be on the lookout for. Throughout, clear line drawings and colour photographs illustrate all the plants.

Written by a team of highly qualified, specialist plantsmen, and laid out for ease of reference, this is the ideal guide for beginner and enthusiast alike.

Part One: Annuals

Introduction

Over a period of many years, a process of careful and methodical selection by plant breeders has enabled gardeners to grow a very wide range of annual, biennial and perennial plants with greater ease than in the past. The frustration of having to wait an age for a plant to flower has been dispelled; most of the varieties included here will bloom in the same season. Other species, which may be biennials or perennials in the wild, will usually flower or produce their decorative foliage within the year, if they are sown early enough, in the same manner as true annuals.

Generally easy to grow, most of them can be used to good effect around the garden and home. There is an excellent variety of containers for yards and patios, and window boxes and hanging baskets may be planted to fill small corners.

Annuals can fill bare gaps that appear after the early-flowering plant subjects, such as bulbs and perennials, have finished flowering. Many kinds can be sown at intervals to give a succession of blooms throughout the season.

F1 hybrids

In recent years much research has gone into the production of a number of new F1 hybrid flowers.

Below: **Dianthus chinensis 'Telstar'**
A beautiful and free-flowering dwarf hybrid which blooms quickly from seed.

Gardeners now enjoy a much wider choice of variety than ever before. Although the seed of F1 hybrids is generally more expensive than that of older kinds, their advantage in colour, flower size, plant habit and general performance are well worth the extra cost of the seed.

In a number of cases these improvements are retained in part in the second generation, called F2 hybrids, which are usually cheaper, but still better than ordinary strains

These hybrids result from first and second generation crosses made between two parent lines specially bred and selected for their ability to produce the desirable qualities that the breeder has in mind, and which go to make a good garden plant. In some instances the introduction of F1 hybrids has almost completely superseded the older cultivars within the space of a few years. The range of species that are bred by this method is gradually extending to enrich still further our homes and gardens.

Propagation

All the types listed in this section are grown from seed. Many of these will not require a greenhouse or frame but can be sown directly where they are to flower. In fact, a number of annuals with small roots or tap-rooted systems do not transplant readily and can best be sown where they are to flower when soil conditions are suitable. Some species that have seeds large enough to handle may be sown direct into small peat pots or other containers; this avoids both pricking off and the risk of root disturbance that may occur when transplanting seedlings.

When the seedlings are being pricked off or transplanted into trays from the containers in which the seed was broadcast, they are best planted with sufficient space to allow development for the planting-out stage. Thin sowings enable this task to be carried out as early as possible, before much root development has taken place.

Outdoor sowings may be either broadcast in patches or put into shallow drills or grooves drawn at intervals to allow for the full development of plants. The drills should be drawn in different directions if more than one kind of seed is sown in a border, so that the groups or patches will look less formal. In both cases the seed should be only lightly covered with fine soil.

Drills will be easier to thin and weed, particularly when weeds begin to be troublesome. Thinning should be a gradual process, done in stages as seedlings develop. On some soils, if difficulty is experienced in making a good seed bed, it may be an advantage to cover seeds with a layer of moistened peat.

As noted under certain species that are hardy, there is often much to be gained, in strength and in earlier flowering, if plants are sown in autumn. In the event of a severe winter killing them, this does give another opportunity to sow in the spring.

Above: **Gazania** x **hybrida 'Ministar'**
These low-growing plants are cultivated for their daisy-shaped flowers, which close up in the evening. They are useful for bedding displays and also as cut flowers for floral arrangements.

Many hardy annuals are admirable for filling in bare places in the garden after the early spring flowering bulbs and plants are finished. Direct sowings should usually start in early springtime, as soon as the soil has become suitably dry.

Position

Because many species need to complete their growth in one season, it is essential to give them the most suitable position possible and to allow room for their full development. A sunny site will suit most but many will tolerate partial shade and a few full shade.

Since heights vary, the taller varieties are best planted towards the back of one-sided borders, or centrally in a more formal area or where the plants may be viewed from various aspects. Those plants which are of intermediate height should be grown nearer the front, and the shortest or most compact kinds of plants are the most suitable for edging the bed or border.

Annual climbers may effectively be used as a background, on trellis or wire mesh, or even as groups grown wigwam fashion; there are many excellent kinds of plastic mesh suited to this purpose. Some kinds of climbers could be used to scramble over a hedge, or old tree stumps, or a bank where little else will grow.

Culture

Failures during all stages of development, from seedling through to flowering, can very often be attributed to such causes as over- or under-watering, or seeds may have been sown too deeply or in unsuitable temperatures; pests and diseases can also take their toll if precautions are not observed and due care is not taken.

Keep the soil just moist throughout their growing life and if possible water seedlings early in the day so that they do not remain wet overnight, which encourages the growth of diseases such as those causing damping-off and root rots.

Watering from above in full sunshine may result in leaf scorch, and drying-out of seeds during germination may kill them. Some shading at this stage is usually beneficial but should be removed before seedlings become drawn or elongated.

A number of excellent seed and growing-on mediums are now readily obtainable, and suitable for growing most kinds of annuals.

The use of suitable greenhouse sprays and smokes as soon as any pests or diseases are observed should ensure healthy plants.

The recommendations for thin sowing, whether indoors or out, must be noted; overcrowded and starved seedlings rarely develop into vigorous plants, and are usually difficult to handle.

Hardening off

This stage of a seedling's life may be critical if sudden changes of temperature occur. Those plants raised in heat and intended for outdoor planting need to be gradually accustomed to lower temperatures and more airy conditions a week or two before planting out. This will depend on the species and the locality.

Tender or half-hardy plants should be protected from the effects of frost or cold winds until late in the spring. A short period in the early stages, during which plants stand in a sheltered position outdoors, helps the hardening-off process and avoids any check in growth that might occur later.

Planting out

The planting area should be prepared well beforehand, working in any necessary addition of compost or fertilizer. Seedlings should be watered a few hours before planting out and also afterwards if the soil is especially dry. Spacing must be sufficient to allow the full development of the species. Of course, cultivation and weeding should be carried out at suitable intervals.

Remove dead flowerheads where possible, to promote continued flowering, and destroy any plants that become affected by disease.

Bob Legge

A-Z Index by Latin Name

Alonsoa warscewiczii

(A. grandiflora)

(Mask flower)

- Sunny location
- Rich and well-drained soil
- Sow in late winter or early spring

Introduced from Peru, this splendid plant grows to a height of 30-60cm/1-2ft. Striking saucer-shaped red flowers are produced on reddish branched stems from summer to late autumn, 2-3cm/0.8-1.25in in diameter. Leaves are ovate and a rich dark green.

Annual in habit, it requires a heated greenhouse for propagation; a temperature of 16°C/60°F, maintained up to planting-out time, will suffice. Sow the seeds in pots of a good growing medium in late winter or early spring. Prick out into boxes or individual pots when the seedlings are large enough. Grow on in gentle heat until late spring. Harden off in the usual way and plant out into permanent positions, approximately 30-40cm/12-15in apart. Choose a sunny position for the best results and make sure the soil is free-draining, otherwise flowers will be disappointing. Stake the plants with bushy twigs if this becomes necessary.

Take care

Do not overwater.

Left: **Alonsoa warscewiczii**

Slender stems of dainty scarlet flowers appear in succession for many weeks during the summer. A sunny position gives best results.

Antirrhinum majus
(Snapdragon)
- **Sunny location**
- **Light to medium soil**
- **Sow in winter to spring**

Because of the introduction of rust-resistant cultivars the snapdragons have now returned to favour. There are many to choose from, either for planting in beds or borders or – the tall types – for use as cut flowers. The range of colours available makes it difficult to choose, but for ordinary garden purposes try the mixture 'Trumpet Serenade'. Having a dwarf bushy habit they are ideal for bedding out from the end of spring onwards. Trumpet-shaped flowers in red, pink, yellow and shades of orange are carried on 30cm/1ft stems. The leaves are a shiny dark green and ovate.

Sow seed on a peat-based growing medium in the late winter or early spring, and lightly cover the seed. Keep in a temperature of 16-21°C/60-70°F. Prick off seedlings in the usual way. Grow on until the end of the spring and then gradually harden off.

Take care
Be sure to use a good quality medium for sowing the seeds.

Argemone mexicana
(Argemony, Devil's fig, Mexican poppy, Prickly poppy)
- **Sunny position**
- **Light and dry soil**
- **Sow in mid-spring**

This unusual annual, introduced from the semi- and tropical areas of America, is, as the name implies, prickly. Extremely majestic orange or yellow flowers will appear from early summer onwards and some protection is given to them by the prickly stems and leaves, the latter being pinnate and glaucous. Some individual flowers can be up to 9cm/3.5in in diameter and being scented they will attract a number of flying insects. Reaching a height of 60cm/2ft the stems are straggly; do not however try to support them, or you will probably do more harm than good.

Sow seeds in boxes of ordinary seed-growing medium in spring at a temperature of 16°C/60°F, prick out into boxes in the usual way and plant into final positions at 30cm/1ft apart in late spring. Alternatively, sow directly into the border in a sunny position during mid-spring, and later thin out to correct spacings.

Take care
Dead-head to prolong flowering.

Above: **Antirrhinum 'Trumpet Serenade'**
An unusual, tubular-flowered mixture of bicoloured blooms with a dwarf bushy habit make ideal bedding subjects.

Left: **Argemone mexicana**
Large, light golden blooms appear against spiny, silvery-green leaves. Grow in a light soil in a sunny position.

Begonia semperflorens

(Wax begonia, Wax plant)

● **Semi-shade or some sun**
● **Light and slightly moist soil**
● **Sow in late winter**

Of all the half-hardy annuals, the begonia must rank high on the list of most gardeners. A very wide range of this group of plants is available: short, tall or medium in height, green or copper foliage, red, pink or white flowers. However, they are tender and therefore some heat will be necessary at propagation time for good results. Plants are usually 15-20cm/6-8in high, with a similar spread.

Sow seeds on a peat-based growing medium in late winter. Mix the seed with a little fine sand before sowing to enable it to be sown more evenly. Do not cover the seed. Place in a temperature of 21°C/70°F. When they are large enough to handle, prick off the seedlings in the usual way. Plant out into final positions in early summer, after the danger of frost has passed.

Take care
Do not plant out too early.

Below: **Begonia semperflorens**
A bushy, much-branched plant with attractive flowers and foliage, the begonia is useful for borders, hanging baskets, and window boxes.

Above: **Borago officinalis**
This tall decorative herb has delightful blue flowers in summer. Young leaves can be used in salads and the dried flowers in pot-pourri.

Borago officinalis
(Borage)
- **Sunny location**
- **Ordinary soil**
- **Sow in mid-spring**

This annual native herb is grown for its foliage and flowers and as a valuable addition to summer salads. Usually attaining a height of 1m/39in, the plants are better suited to the middle or back of a large border; group them together in fours or fives for a bold effect. Larger plants will need staking. The large leaves are obovate, tending to narrow at the base, covered with hairs (as are the long stems), and a good green in colour. Flowers are generally blue, but purple and white forms occur. About 2cm/0.8in across, they resemble five-pointed stars.

This species is very easy to grow. Sow the seeds where the plants are to flower, in mid-spring. Take out small drills and cover the seed. Later thin them out to 30cm/1ft apart. Flowering begins in early summer.

Dried flowers of borage can be used to enhance the ever-popular pot-pourri; blooms are collected before they fully open.

Take care
Clear unwanted seedlings.

Calendula officinalis 'Lemon Gem'
(Pot marigold)
- **Sunny spot**
- **Ordinary free-draining soil**
- **Sow in early spring or autumn**

The very reliable calendulas never cease to delight. The beautiful yellow, orange or gold shades of the flowers are a cheerful sight throughout the season. 'Lemon Gem' has striking double yellow flowers that are formed on compact plants 30cm/1ft high. The long light green leaves are a perfect foil for the bright flowers. Very free-flowering and highly pungent, this plant can be positioned almost anywhere in the garden.

As this is a hardy annual, seeds can be sown where they are to flower during the autumn or early spring. Take out shallow drills and then lightly cover the seed. Thin out to 15cm/6in apart. Alternatively, they can be raised under glass to give uniformity for the formal planting areas. Raise during early spring in a frost-free temperature. Autumn-sown plants will be stronger, and flower earlier.

Take care
Dead-head to prolong flowering.

Below: **Calendula officinalis 'Lemon Gem'**
Double flowers of a beautiful yellow adorn this compact plant throughout the summer. Calendulas are very reliable annuals and can be used in any sunny area of the garden.

Right: **Celosia argentea cristata**
Often used in formal bedding schemes, this distinctive plant can also look effective as a filler in mixed borders. Take care not to overwater.

Celosia argentea cristata
(Cockscomb)
● **Sunny but sheltered position**
● **Rich and well-drained soil**
● **Sow in early spring**

These flowers are unusual in being crested in shape. Colours are red, orange, yellow or pink. Stems are up to 30cm/1ft in height and carry light green ovate leaves. They can be grown outdoors in the summer. Flowers are at their best from early summer onwards, with crests 7-13cm/2.75-5in across.

This tender annual requires heat for good germination. Sow under glass in early spring at a temperature of 16-18°C/60-65°F. Use a reliable seed-growing medium. Prick off seedlings into individual small pots for better results. Harden off carefully about two weeks before required for planting. (Should plants look starved in the pots, give a weak liquid feed weekly up to hardening off.) Plant out in early summer, or late spring in milder areas. Space at 30cm/1ft intervals.

Take care
Overwatering causes collar rot.

Centaurea cyanus 'Red Ball'
(Cornflower)
● **Sunny site**
● **Ordinary well-drained soil**
● **Sow in spring**

This very useful cultivar is an attractive partner to 'Blue Ball' especially if grown for flower arrangements. The individual blooms can be up to 5cm/2in across, deep red and double. The cultivar has been especially selected and bred for earliness, and is more suited to springtime sowing, either directly where it is to flower or under glass.

Make first sowings in the greenhouse in early spring in any good growing medium; prick out into boxes and grow on in reduced temperature; harden off and plant out in late spring. Space out to 30-45cm/12-18in.

'Red Ball' is well worth a place in the annual border, in combination with a selection of plants of similar height.

Take care
Cut off dead flowers in order to encourage new buds and growth.

Left: **Centaurea cyanus 'Red Ball'**
Excellent for cutting, these are dependable plants for a sunny spot. They thrive in an ordinary soil.

Below: **Centaurea cyanus 'Blue Ball'**
An attractive partner for 'Red Ball' in flower arrangements. For a stunning effect grow in bold groups near godetias to give a beautiful contrast.

Centaurea cyanus 'Blue Ball'
(Bachelor's buttons, Bluebottle, Cornflower)
- **Sunny position**
- **Ordinary well-drained soil**
- **Sow in autumn or spring**

The common native cornflower is a great favourite among gardeners, but selection and breeding over many years has led to improved strains for the garden. If you decide to grow this plant, try 'Blue Ball', which is very true to type and is also free from the purple tinge often found in the blues. Strong 90cm/3ft stems carry the ball-like flowers well above the leaves, which are narrow and lanceolate in shape. Grow these flowers in bold groups near godetias and you will have a beautiful contrast of colour throughout the summer months. Cornflowers are often grown as cut flowers either in the border or, alternatively, they can be grown separately in rows in another part of the garden.

Sow the seeds in either the autumn or the spring; those sown in the autumn will make larger plants. Take out drills where the plants are to flower, sow the seed and cover. Thin out subsequent seedlings to 45cm/18in. In very cold areas autumn-sown seedlings should be protected from frost.

Take care
Give support to very tall types.

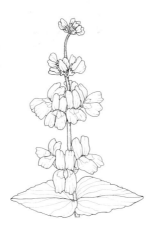

Coix lacryma-jobi

(Job's tears)
● Sunny site
● Any well-drained soil
● Sow in early spring

This is one of a number of annual grasses suitable for beds or borders. The tear-like seeds are grey-green in colour, tiny and pearl-shaped, growing on stems 60-90cm/2-3ft tall. Similar in habit to sweetcorn, they are very vigorous. Once plants are established they will tend to become pendulous before flowering in summer, after which the pearl-like seeds will be formed. If grouped together these plants lend an air of strength to an annual border, and can be accommodated quite happily near very colourful subjects. When ready for harvesting, the hard seeds can be safely used by children for threading on to strings.

Sow seeds in early spring under glass, in a temperature of 13-16°C/55-60°F. Use a loam-based compost and sow directly into individual small pots to save later potting on. Plant out into final positions in early summer.

Take care
Avoid overfeeding, or flowering and seed development will be delayed.

Collinsia bicolor

(C. heterophylla)
● Partial shade
● Moist but well-drained soil
● Sow in autumn or spring

This very appealing hardy annual can be used in most situations as long as they are not too arid. It is a useful plant because it will tolerate partial shade. It is ideal for the border, particularly in a damp shady yard.

Flowers, as its name implies, are two-coloured, having an upper and lower lip formation: the upper petals are usually white and the lower ones lilac to purple. One or two named cultivars are available, mainly pink, and they are worth considering for a change. Their blooms are borne on thin squarish stems carrying lanceolate deep green leaves in pairs. Up to 60cm/2ft in height, they should be grown towards the back of an annual border, preferably near a light yellow subject of a similar height.

Sow seeds where they are to flower, in autumn or spring. Shallow drills will suffice; cover the seeds and thin out, when large enough, to 15cm/6in apart.

Take care
Use bushy peasticks for support.

Above: **Collinsia bicolor**
A pretty annual with tiered sprays of dainty bicoloured flowers. It will grow in a damp, partially shaded position. Be sure to provide support for the slender stems.

Below: **Coix lacryma-jobi**
An annual grass suitable for the bed or border, this plant provides a strong backdrop to more colourful bedding varieties.

Coreopsis tinctoria 'Dwarf Dazzler'

(Calliopsis bicolor)

(Calliopsis, Tickseed)

● **Sunny location**
● **Fertile and well-drained soil**
● **Sow in spring to early summer**

This dwarf cultivar of *Coreopsis* has beautiful daisy-shaped flowers of deep crimson, and each flower is edged with golden yellow, making a vivid contrast. Only 30cm/1ft in height and tending to spread, it is ideally suited to the front of a border or bed in a sunny position. It can also be useful in containers on a patio. An added asset is the remarkable tolerance to smoky environments, and it can therefore be put to good use in industrial towns or cities. Long-lasting and very free-flowering, it should be planted in bold groups in order to achieve the maximum visual effect.

Wherever you choose to grow these plants, they come readily from seed. Sow in spring to early summer where they are to flower; take out shallow drills and cover seed lightly. If you make later sowings and the weather is dry, then water regularly. Thin out seedlings to 30cm/1ft when large enough to handle.

Take care
Sow only when conditions allow.

Right: **Coreopsis tinctoria 'Dwarf Dazzler'**
A reliable dwarf cultivar with masses of crimson and gold flowers in summer, it will tolerate the atmosphere of towns and cities.

Cuphea x purpurea 'Firefly'
(C. miniata)
● Sun or partial shade
● Ordinary soil
● Sow in very early spring

Grown as a half-hardy annual this sub-shrub will do well in most gardens. It spreads to 60cm/2ft and the height is similar. The stems carry green lanceolate leaves, which may be covered with very distinct white hairs. Flowers are formed from the axils of the leaves near the terminals of the stems. Tubular 4cm/1.6in long scarlet blooms will show colour from early summer and it will flower freely throughout that season.

Treat it as a half-hardy annual for propagation purposes. Sow seed under glass in very early spring, using a soil-based growing medium. Cover the seed lightly in boxes or pots and keep in a temperature of 16°C/60°F. Pot off the seedlings into individual small pots and grow on until early summer, when they should be planted out in flowering positions. Give a weak liquid feed once a week in the seedling stages, starting a month after potting on.

Take care
Plant out when frosts are over.

Cynoglossum amabile
(Chinese forget-me-not, Hound's tongue)
● Sun or partial shade
● Rich and well-drained soil
● Sow in early or late spring

This plant has distinctive turquoise-blue flowers like large forget-me-nots. About 45cm/18in high, the stems form a compact plant. Both stems and leaves will be found to have a downy appearance. The flowers usually appear in midsummer. As a biennial it is most useful in a border, especially if you have an odd corner of dappled shade where other plants have difficulty in getting established. If you have, then make sure plenty of humus is added before seed sowing or planting.

Sow the seeds in drills outdoors in late spring to flower the following year, preferably in nursery beds. Plant out seedlings in nursery rows 15cm/6in apart. Set out in final positions at the end of autumn. Alternatively, sow under glass in a temperature of 16°C/60°F during early spring, prick off into boxes or trays, harden off and plant out at the end of spring at 30cm/1ft intervals.

Take care
Do not overwater established plants.

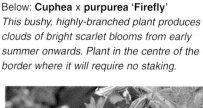

Below: **Cuphea x purpurea 'Firefly'**
This bushy, highly-branched plant produces clouds of bright scarlet blooms from early summer onwards. Plant in the centre of the border where it will require no staking.

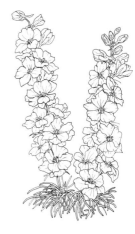

Above: **Cynoglossum amabile**
Useful for a shady spot where other plants experience difficulty in becoming established, the striking blue flowers appear in midsummer.

Below: **Delphinium**
Tall branching sprays of lovely flowers in many shades offer a magnificent display for borders or for household floral arrangements.

Delphinium
(Larkspur)
● **Sheltered and sunny position**
● **Rich and well-cultivated soil**
● **Sow in autumn or spring**

Enjoying a position in a sunny, sheltered border, larkspur will give great pleasure visually, and the innumerable blooms will enable you to cut for arrangements in the house without having any adverse effect on the garden display. Many individual strains and mixtures are available and all are reliable. Colours include blue, purple, pink, white and red. Single or double flowers are produced on erect stems up to 1.2m/4ft tall, in long racemes. The plants spread to about 30cm/1ft and need to be planted towards the back of a border. Leaves are mid-green and deeply cut.

As they are very vigorous in growth, make sure you weed through in the early stages on a regular basis. They can be sown in the open ground in spring, but finer results will be obtained if they are planted in the autumn. Take out drills where plants are to flower, about 30cm/1ft apart, sow seed and cover. Thin out to 30cm/1ft intervals.

Take care
Use peasticks to support tall types.

Right: **Dianthus barbatus**
*These reliable flowers, perfumed with a sweet
scent, are great favourites for cutting and for
summer bedding. They need support to grow to
their full splendour. Red predominates.*

Dianthus barbatus

(Stinking Billie, Sweet William)
- **Sunny location**
- **Avoid very acid soil**
- **Sow in early summer**

The fragrant Sweet William is a useful and
cheerful biennial. The plant ranges in height from
30-60cm/1-2ft; the flowers are produced in a
compact head up to 13cm/5in across. Single or
double blooms open from late spring to early
summer and many colours are available, but red
and white predominate; bicolours are also
common, forming concentric rings in each
individual floret.

Stocky plants can be obtained by sowing
seeds in a prepared seedbed during early
summer. Plant out germinated seedlings into
nursery rows 15cm/6in apart. Keep well weeded
throughout the summer. Final positioning, 20-
25cm/8-10in apart, should be carried out during
the autumn. Alternatively, sow where they are to
flower, in early summer, and thin out to correct
spacing when they are large enough to handle.
Avoid very acid soils and dress with lime before
the final planting if your soil is of this type.

Take care
In exposed situations use bushy twigs to support
the plants.

Left: **Echium lycopsis**
'Monarch Dwarf Hybrids'
A hardy dwarf mixture with flowers of many pleasing pastel shades. Grown in a sunny spot, they will attract hosts of bees in the summer.

Below: **Euphorbia marginata**
Grown for its striking variegated foliage, this plant is well suited to the centre of the border. Superb for flower arrangements when cut.

Echium lycopsis

(E. plantagineum)
(Purple viper's bugloss)
● **Open, sunny location**
● **Light and dry soil**
● **Sow in spring or autumn**

This member of the borage family produces flowers of an upturned bell shape on the end of light green branching stems. The common species is predominantly blue, but 'Monarch Dwarf Hybrids' have blue, lavender, pink, white and carmine shades, and at only 30cm/1ft tall they require no staking and can be used near the front of a border. The mixture is highly recommended. Choose an open sunny site to ensure free-flowering plants, which will open at the end of spring in mild areas and from early summer onwards elsewhere.

In spring sow seeds where plants are to flower; take out shallow drills and lightly cover the seeds. Thin out to 15cm/6in apart. Alternatively, sow seeds in the autumn in the usual way but wait until the springtime before thinning out to final distances.

Take care
Do not overwater when plants are established.

Euphorbia marginata

(Ghost weed, Snow on the mountain)
● **Sun or partial shade**
● **Ordinary soil, or poor if well-drained**
● **Sow in mid-spring**

This annual species originates from North America and is grown mainly for its splendid foliage effect; the flowers are very small, white and insignificant. Stems reach a height of 60cm/2ft. The leaves are ovate or oblong, and a pleasant green but with white margins – the terminal leaves may be completely white in some cases. Bracts beneath the flowers are papery in appearance, and also white. On starved soils the foliage colours are intensified. Use this species towards the centre of a border.

Sow seed directly where it is to flower, in mid-spring; thin out the seedlings to 30cm/1ft spacings. Avoid damaging plants, as the milky latex can have an irritating effect on the skin. This euphorbia is ideally suited for flower arrangements; when cutting, place the ends of the stems in very hot water, as this will have a cauterizing effect and seal the flow of latex.

Take care
Give peastick supports.

Gazania x hybrida
(Treasure flowers)
- **Sunny site**
- **Ordinary well-drained soil**
- **Sow in midwinter**

Without doubt this is one of the finest border, bed or rock garden plants, of an almost exotic nature. However, only in the mildest parts will they survive winter as a perennial, so they are usually treated as an annual.

Hybrid types carry large daisy flowers, and the 'Chansonette' mixture has a colour range including red, bronze and bicolours. Blooms are carried on short stems 20cm/8in long and backed by glossy green leaves, but the undersides of white or silver ensure a contrast.

Most useful as a bedder or planted in full sun on the rock garden, they will give an abundance of flower from early summer onwards.

Sow seed under glass in midwinter in a temperature of 16°C/60°F. Use a loam-based compost for sowing, and prick off individual small pots. Harden off and plant out in early summer, or in late spring in milder areas.

Take care
Make sure ground is free draining to avoid stem and root rots.

Right: **Gazania 'Chansonette'**
A large-flowered hybrid for a sunny position. It will tolerate salty air so it is an ideal plant for seaside gardens.

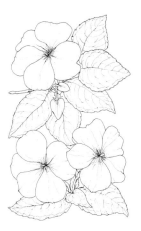

Hibiscus trionum
(Flower of an hour)
- ● Sunny location
- ● Ordinary well-drained soil
- ● Sow in spring

This exquisite half-hardy annual from Africa blooms continuously from midsummer through to the end of autumn. The delicate exotic flowers are up to 7.5cm/3in across, white to pale yellow with a chocolate-maroon centre. Stems bearing these beautiful flowers, up to 75cm/30in long, are a lovely dark green, with ovate leaves that are toothed along the margins. Individual flowers usually last for only one day, but they are eventually followed by an inflated bladder-shaped calyx that will cause interest.

To obtain early-flowering plants, sow seed in pots or boxes in spring; use any good growing medium. When seeds have germinated, prick off seedlings into individual small pots, harden off in a cold frame and plant out at the end of spring. Plants produced in this way will flower earlier than those directly sown in mid-spring. For both methods space the young plants at least 30cm/1ft apart.

Take care
Check young plants for aphids.

Above: **Hibiscus trionum**
Each of these beautiful, creamy flowers lasts for one day only but they appear in succession for many weeks from midsummer until late autumn.

Impatiens
(Busy Lizzie, Touch-me-not)
- ● Shade, semi-shade or sunshine
- ● Ordinary but fertile soil
- ● Sow in mid-spring

During the last decade or so, busy Lizzies have been developed to suit almost any position and conditions. They are very versatile, and can be safely used in difficult shady parts of the garden or in full sunshine: not many half-hardy annuals tolerate both.

So many cultivars or hybrids are available that it is difficult to make a choice, but the very dwarf 'Novette' mixture, with plants only 10cm/4in high, is well worth considering.

As a tender half-hardy annual, it will need to be raised under glass. Sow seed on a peat-based growing medium and lightly cover, in spring. Keep at a temperature of 18°C/65°F; if it falls below this, then germination will be difficult and uneven. When they are large enough to handle, prick out the seedlings into boxes of a peat-based growing medium. Harden off gradually and plant out into their final growing positions in early summer.

Take care
Do not plant out too early.

Right: **Impatiens 'Novette' F1 Mixed**
A colourful mixture of glistening flowers for shady, semi-shaded or sunny spots in the garden or on the patio. Plants grow to 10cm/4in with a wide spread.

Lathyrus odoratus
(Sweet pea)
- Sunny but sheltered location
- Well-drained medium loam
- Sow in autumn or spring

For ordinary garden purposes let sweet peas ramble over trellis work or arches, or provide a wigwam of peasticks for support in the annual or mixed border or bed.

Dig in plenty of organic matter before planting, to provide for a cool root run by retaining moisture at the hottest times of the year. Sow the seeds (peas) in autumn or spring; those sown in autumn will flower earlier. To help the seed to germinate, nick the hard outer casing of the seed or soak it in water for 24 hours before sowing in a loam-based growing medium. Use pots or boxes for sowing and then place the seedlings singly in small pots. Autumn sowings need to be placed in a cold frame; those sown in spring must be kept in a temperature of 16°C/60°F. Plant out in early spring, 15cm/6in apart.

Take care
Remove faded flowers regularly.

Left: **Lathyrus odoratus 'Sheila MacQueen'**
A lovely sweet pea with large waved flowers for exhibition and cutting. Be sure to provide plenty of organic matter in the soil and remove faded flowers regularly.

Lupinus hartwegii
(Lupin)
- **Sun or partial shade**
- **Neutral or acid and poor soil**
- **Sow in autumn or spring**

Handsome spikes of this popular annual will give long-lasting colour in the average garden throughout the summer. 'Pixie Delight' will give shades of pink, purple, blue and red, on stems 45cm/18in high, from early summer to late autumn. The plants of this mixture do not need staking. Frequently used to fill gaps in mixed or herbaceous borders, they look just as well in a bed or border on their own. Plant them also in containers for the patio or yard. An abundance of seedpods can be produced and it is wise to remove these if you have young children, as tummy upsets may occur if they eat the small peas or pods. To be safe, cut off the flowerhead as soon as the colour has faded.

Plants are easily raised from seeds, sown directly where they are to flower in autumn or spring. Autumn-sown plants will be earlier to flower and somewhat larger. Thin out seedlings to 23cm/9in apart.

Take care
Fork peat into an alkaline soil.

Matthiola incana 'Dwarf Ten Week Stock'
- **Sun or partial shade**
- **Most soils, preferably alkaline**
- **Sow in spring**

These flowers, on 25cm/10in stems, and in a splendid range of red, pink, rose, carmine and purple, will be long lasting. Blooms will appear about 10 days before other cultivars of the type. Correct cultural conditions are essential to obtain maximum results. Sow under glass in the early spring at a temperature of 18-21°C/65-70°F. Use a sterile growing medium in order to avoid damping-off disease. When germination has been completed reduce the temperature to 10°C/50°F.

If you grow the selectable strains, you can discard the dark types and prick off the light ones; this will ensure that most will be double-flowered. When handling young seedlings, hold them by the edge of a leaf and not by the sensitive stem, which could be damaged and subsequently rot. Plant out after hardening off, at 23cm/9in intervals.

Take care
It is advisable to add lime to the soil before planting if it is too acid.

Above: **Lupinus hartwegii 'Pixie Delight'**
A dwarf form of annual lupin with pretty mixed flowers that will provide colour well into autumn. These plants will not need support.

Right: **Matthiola incana 'Dwarf Ten Week Stock'**
Flowering earlier than other cultivars of this type, these splendid purple blooms offer a dramatic splash of colour.

Above: **Matthiola incana 'Giant Imperial Mixed'**
This is a fine mixture of these sweetly scented garden favourites. The flowering stems will grow to a height of about 50cm/20in.

Nicandra physaloides
(Apple of Peru. Shoo fly plant)
- Sunny position
- Rich well-cultivated soil
- Sow in early spring

This is a very strong annual, up to 1m/39in in height. The pale blue bell-shaped flowers, 4cm/1.6in long, have a contrasting white throat. The flower is followed by a non-edible green apple-shaped fruit encased in a five-winged purple calyx. Stems tend to be branched and spreading; the finely toothed leaves have wavy edges and are a pleasant green. Because of their ultimate size these plants require plenty of room to develop, and they are best used towards the back of an annual or mixed border, preferably in full sun. Before planting, fork in plenty of organic matter.

This unusual annual is easily grown from seed. Sow under glass in early spring at a temperature of 16°C/60°F. Use a good growing medium for sowing and potting. Put seedlings into individual small pots and grow on in the same temperature. Harden off in the usual way and plant out in early summer, 30cm/1ft apart.

Take care
Support individual specimens.

Matthiola incana 'Giant Imperial Mixed'
- Sunny position but tolerates partial shade
- Most soils, preferably alkaline
- Sow in early spring

This must be one of the most popular scented annuals. *En masse* this fragrance can be overpowering, however, so do not overplant. The 'Giant Imperial' mixture always provides reliable flowers with a high percentage of doubles. Stems 38-50cm/15-20in tall carry a profusion of pink, white, lilac, purple and crimson spikes of flowers from early summer onwards. Grey-green soft narrow leaves are formed under the flowerheads and give a pleasing contrast.

Sow seed for summer flowering during the early spring under glass in a temperature of 13°C/55°F. Use a loam-based mixture for sowing and pricking off seedlings. Grow on in a lower temperature, and harden off before planting out 23cm/9in apart.

Take care
Kill caterpillars at once.

Below: **Nicandra physaloides**
This tall, branching annual should be given adequate space to develop. The flowers are produced over many weeks but open only for a few hours during the middle of the day.

Nicotiana tabacum

(N. gigantea)

(Tobacco plant)

● **Sunny position**
● **Rich well-drained soil**
● **Sow in early spring**

The true tobacco plant can reach a height of 2m/6.5ft and therefore if you are thinking of this plant for an ornamental effect in the garden the choice of site will need to be carefully considered. Large leaves up to 1m/39in long are borne on strong stems. Dull red or pink flowers of a funnel shape usually appear from midsummer until autumn. Use these plants in groups at the back of an annual border as an architectural feature, or in large containers on a patio. The leaves will change from green to a light golden colour towards autumn.

Sow under glass in early spring, in a temperature of 18°C/65°F. Use any good growing medium. Prick off into individual small pots and grow on. Give a weak liquid feed up to hardening-off time, about every 10 days.

Plant out in early summer at intervals of 60-90cm/2-3ft. A sheltered sunny site will avoid the necessity for staking, especially if plants are grouped together.

Take care

Spray against aphids.

Right: **Nicotiana tabacum**
Tall plants such as these are ideal for planting in groups at the back of the border. They are best grown in a sheltered and sunny position.

Papaver rhoeas

(Corn poppy, Field poppy, Flanders poppy, Poppy)

● **Sunny location**
● **Light well-drained soil**
● **Sow in autumn or spring**

From the common wild scarlet field poppy, the Rev. W. Wilks made his famous selections from which, in the 1880s, the world-renowned Shirley poppy strain was introduced. Mainly in the range of pink, red and white, a number will be found to be bicoloured or picotee. Double strains now exist, but the single type are more allied to the original introductions. This very worthy annual is hardy, and can be used in borders and in the odd pocket towards the back of a rock garden, as long as the position is sunny.

Up to 60cm/2ft in height, the stems carry lovely deeply-lobed leaves above which the flowers are borne, about 7.5cm/3in across.

Sow seeds in spring or autumn. Take out shallow drills where the plants are to flower. Sow seeds and lightly cover with soil. Thin out seedlings to 30cm/1ft apart. Flowers appear in early summer.

Take care
Spray against aphids.

Right: **Papaver rhoeas**
These very decorative poppies provide a short-lived but extremely colourful show in the early part of the summer.

28

Perilla nankinensis
(P. frutescens)
- Sunny site
- Ordinary well-cultivated soil
- Sow in very early spring

Grown for its beautiful bronze-purple foliage, this half-hardy annual is most useful as a spot plant in formal bedding schemes or as an architectural plant in the mixed or annual border. If you have a patio surrounded by a light-coloured wall, large containers of this plant will provide a unique and striking contrast.

The showy leaves are toothed, ovate and pointed. When bruised, these and the insignificant white flowers emit a spice-like fragrance, reminiscent of their Chinese origin. Given good growing conditions, plants will reach a height of 60cm/2ft.

Propagate under glass in very early spring. Sow seeds in pots or boxes of a good growing medium. Keep in a temperature of 18°C/65°F. Prick off the seedlings into individual pots. Harden off and plant out in early summer. If growing together in groups allow 30cm/1ft between plants.

Take care
Stake individual specimens.

Phlox drummondii
- Open and sunny site
- Ordinary well-drained soil
- Sow in spring

Easy-to-grow half-hardy annuals, *P. drummondii* will give a succession of colour throughout the summer. For a really bright display try the cultivar 'Carnival'; this mixture has pink, rose, salmon, scarlet, blue and violet flowers. These are borne on stems 30cm/1ft high, carrying light green lanceolate leaves. Blooms are produced in early summer as dense heads up to 10cm/4in in diameter; each individual flower is rounded. These plants are ideally suited for low-growing areas of the garden, especially the rock garden, where pockets can be filled to give a constant show of colour.

In spring, sow seeds under glass in a temperature of 16°C/60°F. Use any good growing medium for sowing. Sow the seeds thinly and cover them lightly. Prick off the young seedlings, when they are large enough to handle, into boxes or trays. Harden off and plant them out in their flowering positions in the early summer at 23cm/9in intervals.

Take care
Dead-head to prolong flowering.

Above: **Phlox drummondii 'Carnival'**
This sweetly scented dwarf mixture includes many lovely colours with contrasting eyes for a really bright display throughout the summer.

Left: **Perilla nankinensis**
This half-hardy annual provides a rich backdrop of bronze-purple foliage and is useful as an architectural plant in the mixed border.

Above: **Portulaca grandiflora**
*In dry sunny situations these fleshy-leaved
plants will abound with bright flowers during the
summer. Water established plants sparingly.*

Portulaca grandiflora
(Eleven o'clock, Rose moss, Sun plant)
- Full sun
- Ordinary well-drained soil
- Sow in spring

Originating from Brazil, portulacas have now
come into their own as worthwhile plants for the
annual border or (more especially) for pockets in
the rock garden. In some areas they can be
temperamental but given a good sunny site they
should thrive well on most soils. The flowers of *P.
grandiflora* are produced on semi-prostrate
stems of a reddish colour, usually up to 23cm/9in
in height. Red, purple, rose, orange-scarlet,
yellow and white, the blooms can be over
2.5cm/1in across. Each centre has pronounced
yellow stamens. The leaves are round and fleshy.

Sow seed in early spring under glass, in a
temperature of 18°C/65°F. Use any good growing
medium for this purpose and for the subsequent
pricking-off of seedlings. Harden off in a cold
frame and plant out in early summer, 15cm/6in
apart. Alternatively, sow outside in mid-spring.

Take care
Water established plants only in extreme
temperatures.

Ricinus communis
(Castor oil plant)
- Sunny location
- Ordinary well-cultivated soil
- Sow in early spring

Treated as a half-hardy annual for normal
garden work, this species originates from Africa.

Grown for the beautiful large palmate leaves
up to 30cm/1ft across, castor oil plants are best
used at the back of an informal border to give
height and character. Depending on the cultivar
the leaves will be green, purple or bronze. Petal-
less flowers are produced in summer, followed
by large spiky round seedpods. Beware because
these seedpods can be poisonous if the internal
seeds are eaten.

Sow seeds in early spring in a heated
greenhouse at a temperature of 21°C/70°F. Sow
in individual pots of a good growing medium.
Move the seedlings on into larger pots
(10cm/4in) and reduce the temperature to
10°C/50°F. Harden off the plants in a cold frame
for at least two weeks before planting them out
in the early summer.

Take care
Staking will be necessary.

Rudbeckia hirta
(Black-eyed Susan, Coneflower)
● **Sunny position**
● **Any soil**
● **Sow in spring**

The common names of this species (Black-eyed Susan and Coneflower) allude to the centre of the flower, which has a very dark brown to purple colour and is cone-shaped. The outer petals are lovely shades of yellow, gold and brown. Recommended is the cultivar 'Marmalade' which is a rich yellow with a central cone of purple-black – very striking. It flowers from the early summer, and blooms will be carried in great profusion until the late autumn on stems 45cm/18in long. Individual flowers will be up to 10cm/4in across.

To obtain flowering plants each year, sow seeds in boxes of any good growing medium in spring. Heat will not be required and they can be raised in either a cold greenhouse or a frame. Prick out the young seedlings into boxes and place these in a cold frame to protect them from frosts. Harden off in late spring and plant out into flowering positions in very early summer, 23cm/9in apart.

Take care
Watch out for slug damage.

Above: **Ricinus communis**
These stately plants add height and interest to the border. Plant in the early summer and provide support.

Below: **Rudbeckia hirta 'Marmalade'**
These long-lasting golden flowers are borne on tall stems and appear from early summer though to the late autumn.

Salvia horminum
(Clary)

- **Sunny position**
- **Ordinary well-drained soil**
- **Sow in early spring or autumn**

This plant from southern Europe will provide a completely different range of colour from the *S. splendens* scarlet cultivars. Dark blue or purple bracts are produced around the insignificant true flowers. Mixtures are available, but the cultivar 'Blue Beard' is recommended for its very deep purple bracts on erect branching square stems, 45cm/18in high. These also carry the ovate mid-green leaves. Grow towards the front of a border, or as a formal bedding plant with a few silver spot plants.

These hardy annuals may be sown direct outdoors in spring or autumn. If earlier colour is required plants can be raised under glass by sowing in seed mixture in spring at a temperature of 18°C/65°F. Prick off into individual pots or seed trays. Grow on cooler and harden off to plant out at 23cm/9in apart in early summer. Too high temperatures will produce soft elongated growth.

Take care
Thin seedlings sown outdoors before they become crowded.

Right: **Salvia horminum**
The striking blue or purple bracts surround the true flowers, which are insignificant. Grow these attractive plants in well-drained soil in a sunny location for best results.

Above: **Salvia sclarea**
This is a useful plant for a large border, both for its bold foliage and for its elegant sprays of true flowers and showy bracts. Grow this biennial in sun on light soil.

Salvia sclarea
(Clary)
- Full sun
- Light and fertile soil
- Sow in spring

This handsome biennial was grown in the past for use as a culinary herb but is now surpassed by the various species of sage. The oil, however, is still extracted commercially for use in the manufacture of perfumes. Reaching a height of 75cm/30in, the stems carry large, very hairy triangular leaves of mid-green. Flowers are tubular in shape, about 2.5cm/1in long, and white-blue in colour. Below the true flowers, bracts of purple or yellow will accentuate the whole blooms, which show colour from midsummer onwards. These are good border plants, which will enhance an otherwise flat area; use them towards the back of the border.

This species is biennial in habit. The seeds are sown in spring where they are to flower. Take out drills 38cm/15in apart; thin out seedlings to 30cm/1ft apart when they are large enough to handle.

Take care
Use leaves for culinary purposes from midsummer onwards.

Silybum marianum
(Our Lady's milk thistle)
- Sunny and open site
- Any soil
- Sow in spring or autumn

Beautiful thistle flowers of a violet colour are produced in late summer by this lovely plant from the Mediterranean. More often than not, though, it is grown for its remarkable foliage; the attractive dark green leaves are mottled or flecked with white. Ovate in shape, they carry spines in and around the lobes. Stems carrying the flowers can be up to 1.5m/5ft in height and arise from rosettes of the beautiful glossy leaves. Use this as an architectural plant at the back of a mixed, annual or herbaceous border.

Stronger plants will be obtained if seed is sown in autumn rather than in the spring. In either case take out drills where the plants are to be effective. Sow the seed and lightly cover over. Thin out the young seedlings as early as possible, to 60cm/2ft apart. Despite their height these plants should not require staking. In fact, this practice should be avoided or the overall visual effect can be spoiled.

Take care
Give plants enough space.

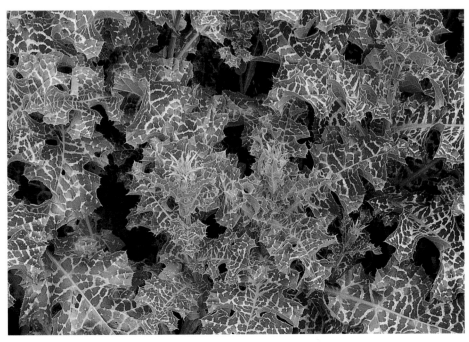

Right: **Silybum marianum**
Grow these striking plants at the back of the border, where their bold green leaves flecked with white add height and interest. Thistle flowers appear in late summer.

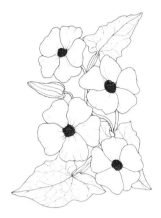

Tagetes patula
(Dwarf French marigold)
- **Sunny position**
- **Ordinary soil**
- **Sow in spring**

Rather a misnomer, the French marigold originates from Mexico. The number of cultivars to choose from increases each year; the recent introduction 'Silvia' is a dwarf form of the species, growing only 20cm/8in high. The large yellow blooms are remarkably resistant to unfavourable weather conditions. These compact plants are ideal subjects for edging around formal beds and borders. They are also very useful for the front of window boxes and other containers on a patio or in a yard. In such conditions water well.

As half-hardy annuals, these plants need to be raised under glass. Sow seed in spring, in pots or boxes of any good growing medium. Keep in a temperature of 18°C/65°F. Germination is usually very quick, and pricking out should be done as soon as the young seedlings are manageable. Harden off and plant out in early summer, at 23cm/9in intervals.

Take care
Keep established plants on the dry side unless they are in containers.

Thunbergia alata
(Black-eyed Susan, Clock vine)
- **Sunny and sheltered position**
- **Ordinary well-drained soil**
- **Sow in spring**

Surely one of the finest annual climbers, the clock vine comes from the southern part of Africa. It freely produces 5cm/2in wide tubular flowers of orange-yellow, the centre of the tube being dark purple-brown. Blooms are formed from the axils of the ovate light green leaves, which are carried on twining stems up to 3m/10ft long. This is an ideal climbing plant for the cool greenhouse. If given a sheltered sunny site it will do equally well in the garden: grow it against a wall, or on tall peasticks in an annual or mixed border. If space and position allow, let this species twine amongst a blue clematis – a lovely combination.

Sow seeds in spring under glass in a temperature of 16-18°C/60-65°F: use any good growing medium. Prick off the seedlings singly into individual small pots and place a split cane in each to give support. Plant out after hardening off in summer.

Take care
Keep young plants well spaced under glass to prevent tangling.

Verbena x hybrida
(V. hortensis)
(Vervain)
- **Sunny position**
- **Any fertile soil**
- **Sow in early spring**

This is a half-hardy perennial usually grown as a half-hardy annual. There are numerous varieties of this bushy plant, in a range of colours including white, pink, red, blue and lilac. Heights range from 15-45cm/6-18in. They are ideal subjects for growing in borders, on the rock garden and also in containers, providing an attractive focal point.

Sow the seeds in pots or boxes in early spring under glass. Keep at a constant temperature of 16°C/60°F. Use any good growing medium. Prick off the young seedlings, as soon as they are ready, into boxes or trays. Harden off and plant out into their flowering positions in early summer. Those intended for display in containers and window boxes can be planted out slightly earlier than this as long as they are situated in sheltered positions. Water freely in very dry weather.

Take care
It is important to water these plants generously during dry, hot spells.

Left: **Tagetes patula 'Silvia'**
With superb yellow blooms, these compact plants are ideal for edging the formal bed or border and are also suitable for window boxes and other containers.

Above: **Thunbergia alata**
This vigorous annual climber will grow well outdoors in a sunny and sheltered spot. The pretty flowers are freely produced throughout the summer. Provide support.

Left: **Verbena 'Florist Mixed'**
A bright mixture with a wide range of colours, many showing contrasting eyes. Grow this dwarf verbena on the rock garden, at border edges, and in containers and window boxes.

35

Part Two: Perennials

Introduction

What is a perennial plant? All plants are perennials except annuals and biennials. In this section the term perennial indicates herbaceous or hardy herbaceous perennials. This includes hardy plants and some half-hardy ones whose foliage dies back each autumn or winter after flowering and returns to life in the spring, when new young shoots emerge from a clump of dead-looking material. However, perennials are not always deciduous: for example, *Heuchera* and *Liriope* have evergreen foliage, and they will provide interest during the winter months.

Some of the terms I use here might bewilder a beginner so perhaps a word of explanation might be in order. A *wilding* is a wild plant, flower or fruit. A *panicle* is a flowerhead with several branches, each having a number of stalked flowers. A *truss* is a flower-cluster at the top of a stem, as in *Phlox*. An *umbel* is several stems and flowers arising from a main stem or shoot, shaped like an upturned umbrella. *Deciduous* plants die down or lose their foliage in winter. *Humus* is any organic matter, such as leaves, plant stems or animal refuse, when decayed. *Leaf-mould* is decayed or rotted leaves; the best is of oak or beech leaves. Rotted garden *compost* consists of a mixture of decaying foliage and stems from herbaceous plants, material from the vacuum cleaner bag,

kitchen waste, but not potato peelings, as these can grow and produce potatoes. Also, whenever available, use well-rotted farmyard manure, cow manure, or pig manure; on a heavy clay soil, horse manure is suitable.

General cultivation

As long as you have the strength and will-power to dig, do so. Initial preparation of the soil always pays dividends. When preparing a new bed or border I bastard-trench or double dig. To do this take out the first spit or two of top soil (a spit is one spade's depth), then fork over the bottom spit of sub-soil and cover with the next one or two top spits. When digging, remove all pernicious weeds such as bindweed, ground elder, docks and dandelions – these are known to some gardeners as malignant weeds. Once these irritants are removed, the bed or border has been properly dug with humus incorporated, and the soil has settled, the ground is ready for planting. Always plant firmly and use a hand-fork to make the hole, rather than a trowel. Humus can be well-rotted garden compost, well-rotted farmyard manure or leaf-mould. Initial preparation is paramount, for once the plants are in the ground there is little one can do, though a gardener I knew mulched all around his plants each year with farmyard manure. Today many gardeners use pulverized bark as a mulch

to prevent the soil from drying out during summer, and this also acts as a good weed preventative.

Many plants require ample moisture during hot, dry weather. Spray them with clear water in the evening after sunset. Where water has to be applied to the roots of plants, apply a mulch of rotted garden compost or farmyard manure to prevent evaporation.

Stakes and supports

Not all perennials require staking or support; many are sturdy enough to remain upright. But for those that do require some form of support, staking should be carried out at the start of the season, before growth has become too advanced. Peasticks are excellent if inserted in and around the plants or clumps so that the new growth can grow through them; when the plants come into flower the supports are well camouflaged.

Today there are special plant supports for herbaceous border plants; neither sticks nor string is required, just a stout wire stake that supports a galvanized wire ring 20-25cm/8-10in wide, and

Below: **Aster amellus 'Rudolph Goethe'**
This has rough-textured, grey-green leaves. Its mauve flowers appear during the middle of the summer and it is best planted in bold groups for a striking splash of colour.

Above: Phlox paniculata 'Rijnstroom'
These plants are suitable for both mixed borders and for cutting to use in floral displays. The flowers are carried in dense clusters and occur in varying shades of pink.

the plants grow through them so that the supports are rendered almost invisible. Other types are a triangle with three supports, or a ring with cross pieces and three supports.

Beds and borders

The traditional herbaceous border was planted rather like a shop window, with short, medium and tall plants ranging from front to back. Usually at the back of the border there was a wall, fence or hedge, often a yew hedge. Some gardeners now plant perennials in island beds cut out of a lawn, and this is an ideal method for a small garden because it gets rid of rigid straight lines. Island beds can be round, oval or rectangular. By this method the gardener can get right round the bed.

Choice of plants

Most gardeners have their favourite plants that they wish to grow. Remember that a bed or border can look rather dull during the late autumn and winter, and this can be partly avoided by growing a few clumps of plants that retain their foliage throughout the year – plants such as *Liriope* and *Heuchera*. To add interest a few shrubs can be included along with the herbaceous plants, such as helianthemums, *Ruta graveolens* 'Jackman's Blue', *Rosmarinus* 'Jessop's Upright', *Senecio* 'Sunshine', *Hypericum elatum* 'Elstead Variety', *Lavandula* 'Hidcote Blue', *Hebe pinguifolia* 'Pagei', *Euonymus* 'Emerald 'n Gold', or perhaps *Berberis thunbergii* 'Aurea'.

When you are planning a border or island bed, remember that many plants look more effective when planted in groups of three, four or five to the square metre or yard. In a small garden, however, some plants are best grown alone.

Propagation

A vast number of perennials can be increased from seed and in many cases the seedling plants will be like their parents. In other instances they will vary in colour. Some varieties produce a surprisingly wide range of colours from a single packet of seed. Therefore with many plants it will be necessary to divide them to retain a desirable colour, in either autumn or spring.

Division can be performed in several ways: pull a plant apart with the hands; cut through it with a stout sharp knife; use two hand-forks, placing them back to back, then grip the handles together and ease the plant apart gradually.

Plants such as poppies can be increased by taking root cuttings during the autumn or winter months. This can be done by cutting the roots into approximately 3-5cm/1.2-2in lengths, making a horizontal cut at the top and a slanting cut at the base to avoid inserting the cuttings upside down. Where cuttings are up to 5cm/2in long, a box will need to be 8cm/3.2in deep. Fill the box with a mixture of 1 part medium loam, 2 parts granulated peat and 3 parts coarse silver sand (all parts by volume); no fertilizers are required with this mixture. I have used this mixture many times but if peat has not been available I have used well-rotted oak or beech leaf-mould. Today many growers use a soil-less mixture, which is fine; when the cuttings are rooted they can be potted or lined out in a nursery row.

When using peat, make sure it is properly moistened before mixing it with loam and sand; unless this is done, water will not be soaked up afterwards. When using pots, boxes or pans, always make certain that they are clean before use, and well crocked by placing broken pieces of pot and dry leaves in the bottom of the container to ensure good drainage. When using soil-less mixtures, crocks are not necessary, and the mixture must not be made too firm.

Pests and diseases

Perhaps the worst pest – apart from a cat scratching around newly cultivated soil – is the slug, which adores luscious new shoots. Today there are plenty of slug-killers on the market. Snails also do damage, especially to new young shoots. Another very common pest is the greenfly or aphid. To control these, spray or dust with pyrethrum or malathion. The best way to avoid phlox eelworm – a small pest that cannot be seen by the naked eye – is to increase phlox from root cuttings taken from clean stock. Phlox roots are rather like bootlaces. Cut them into 8cm/3.2in lengths, lay them on a cuttings mixture, and cover them. Another pest that often causes havoc is the Solomon's seal sawfly, which disfigures foliage by chewing it to pieces. Control by hand picking, or by spraying with malathion. Ants, too, can be a considerable nuisance; pyrethrum will help to control them, but there are also various specific ant-killers available on the market.

Noël Prockter

A-Z Index by Latin Name

Achillea millefolium 'Cerise Queen'

(Milfoil, Yarrow)
● **Sunny position**
● **Well-drained soil**
● **Summer flowering**

Although the common yarrow *A. millefolium* can become a headache to the lawn purist, the variety 'Cerise Queen' is quite attractive. It has wide flattish heads of rose-cerise flowers, each floret with a paler centre, on stout 60cm/2ft stems in summer. The dark green feathery foliage makes a mat-like plant. It is ideal for the front of the border, but gardeners beware – it can become invasive.

Propagate either by sowing seed in spring in a cold house or frame, or by taking cuttings in early summer, again in a cold house or frame, or by division in autumn. A few stout peasticks inserted around the plants will prevent them being blown over in windy gardens.

There are many varieties which will grace any border or bed with summer colour. For best results they should be planted in well-drained soil in a sunny position.

Take care
Plant this species in a sheltered spot, if possible.

Right: **Agapanthus 'Headbourne Hybrids'**
These beautiful plants are hardy, except in the coldest and wettest areas. Their handsome flowers, in varying shades of blue, are borne on stout stems up to 90cm/3ft high.

Left: **Achillea millefolium 'Cerise Queen'**
*A lovely plant for the front of the border. The flat
flowerheads are carried on stems 60cm/2ft tall
and may need support.*

Agapanthus
(African lily)
● **Sunny position**
● **Moist and fertile soil**
● **Summer flowering**

The blue African lily, *Agapanthus umbellatus*,
belongs to the family Liliaceae, but is not, in fact,
a lily; it is hardy outdoors only in gardens that
are usually frost-free. Today, however, there are
some very fine garden forms that are hardy.
During the 1950s and 1960s the 'Headbourne
Hybrids' were developed from *A. campanulatus*;
they are in varying shades of blue.

All agapanthus plants have lily-like flowers that
are arranged in an umbel, which looks like an
upturned umbrella. The flowers are borne on
stoutish stems, 60-90cm/2-3ft high. They are
deciduous, and the dark green strap-like foliage
dies down in the winter, so it is wise to mark the
spot where they grow so that when the border is
dug over, the plants are not damaged. Choose
moist rather than dry soil, but it is advisable to
avoid very wet ground.

Propagate by division in spring, as the new
growth appears.

Take care
Avoid deep planting.

Anaphalis yedoensis
(Everlasting, Life-everlasting, Pearly everlasting)
● **Sun or partial shade**
● **Well-drained soil**
● **Late summer or autumn flowering**

This plant has broad green leaves that are
white-felted beneath, and flat papery white
flowerheads with enchanting yellow centres.
These develop from late summer through to
early autumn, reaching up to 10cm/4in across
each flowerhead. Although its foliage dies back
in the winter, silvery-white shoots soon appear
as spring approaches. The plant will eventually
reach a height of 60cm/2ft.

When pearly everlasting flowers are gathered
for drying, for use in winter flower arrangements,
give the stems a good drink before hanging
them up to dry off. *A. yedoensis* is best when
grown in full sun, although it can tolerate the
shade of a wall (but not of trees).

Propagate by division in autumn, or by seeds
sown out of doors in spring. Plant them in any
good retentive soil.

Take care
These plants will soon droop if they become too
dry at the roots, so it is important to ensure they
are kept moist at all times.

Below: **Anaphalis yedoensis**
*The papery white 'everlasting' flowers are
carried on stems 60cm/2ft tall above broad
green leaves that are white-felted beneath. Soak
the stems before drying in winter.*

Anemone x hybrida

(A. japonica)

(Windflower)

● **Sun or partial shade**
● **Good ordinary soil**
● **Early autumn flowering**

Of all the many windflowers, the best-known are the many hybrids of the Japanese anemones *A. x hybrida* (also known as *A. japonica*). These vary in height from 45-120cm/18-48in, and their individual flowers vary in size from 4-6 cm/1.6-2.4in across, each with five or more petals. Each flower has a central boss of yellow stamens. The stems are clothed with vine-like leaves. Their roots are like stiff black leather bootlaces. Choose from the following selection: 'Bressingham Glow', a semi-double rosy-red, 45cm/18in tall; 'Luise Uhink', white, 90cm/3ft; 'White Queen', 90-120cm/3-4ft; and 'Honorine Jobert', white, 120cm/4ft.

Propagate by cutting the roots into 4-5cm/1.6-2in lengths and inserting them in a deep box filled with peat and sand mixture.

Take care

Good drainage is needed, and preferably in a sunny position.

Right: Aruncus dioicus
This handsome and tenacious hardy herbaceous perennial has magnificent plumes of creamy-white flowers in the summer. Grow it in some shade in deep fertile soil.

Left: **Anemone 'Honorine Jobert'**
This lovely white form was a 'sport' from a red-flowered variety in the garden of M. Jobert, in 1858. It thrives in sun or partial shade.

Aster x frikartii 'Mönch'
- **Sunny position**
- **Good well-drained soil**
- **Summer to autumn flowering**

Aster x frikartii 'Mönch' is a hybrid between *A. amellus* and *A. thomsonii*. Its flowering period is considerably longer than *A. amellus* varieties. 'Mönch' has stout branching stems up to 90cm/3ft bearing an abundance of clear lavender-blue flowers with yellow rayed centres, lasting until the frosts begin in autumn. Every collection of hardy herbaceous perennials should possess a few examples of this plant.

Grow this hybrid aster in well-drained soil in an open sunny position. Make sure that there is sufficient moisture in the soil to sustain the autumn flowers but avoid excessive wetness during the winter months.

Propagate this variety by basal cuttings in spring, or by division where possible. It is best planted in spring.

Take care
This plant must not have a wet rootstock in the winter months.

Aruncus dioicus
(A. sylvester)
(Goat's beard)
- **Sunshine or shade**
- **Deep, rich and fertile soil**
- **Summer flowering**

Goat's beard has had its botanical name changed several times, but nurserymen still use the name *A. sylvester*. It is a tall and rather handsome plant, with broad fern-like foliage on stiff wiry stems, 120-150cm/4-5ft tall; above are impressive plumes of creamy-white stars throughout the summer.

Plants make bold hummocks, which need a great deal of strength to lift out of the ground once they are well established, and even more strength when division is necessary. They do better in a deep, fertile soil with some shade.

The male and female flowers are on different plants; the male flowers are more feathery than the female ones, and they are not so troublesome by germinating self-sown seedlings. Even so, the female seedheads come into their own for drying. Propagate by spring-sown seed or divide clumps in late autumn.

Take care
Male plants are more free-flowering than the female plants.

Below: **Aster x frikartii Mönch**
A splendid hybrid that blooms earlier and for a longer period than other varieties. Its 75cm/30in stems carry lavender-blue flowers well into the autumn months.

Astilbe x arendsii

(False goat's beard, Perennial spiraea)
- Sunshine or partial shade
- Moist fertile soil
- Summer flowering

Astilbes are one of our most decorative hardy herbaceous perennials. The arendsii hybrids vary from white, through pale pink, deep pink, coral and red, to magenta. Not only are they good garden plants but they also force well under glass in an unheated greenhouse. The foliage varies from light to dark green, with some of the purplish and reddish-purple shades. The fluffy panicles of flowers are held on erect stems 60-90cm/2-3ft tall, but the dwarf varieties are only 45cm/18in.

They will grow in full sun or partial shade and thrive in most soils. They have a long flowering period and their rigid erect stems do not require staking. There are too many varieties to mention, but all are worth a place in any garden.

Propagate by division in spring. Alternatively, roots may be divided in autumn and potted for forcing or spring planting.

Take care
Do not cut old flower stems back before spring.

Above: **Astilbe** x **arendsii**
These hardy herbaceous perennials are ideal in a garden where the soil does not dry out. Astilbes flower over a long period and do not need to be staked. Good for sun or shade.

Above: **Astrantia major**
For those who favour 'everlasting' flowers the paper-like florets of the astrantias are very attractive. Suited to dappled shade.

Astrantia major
(Masterwort)
- **Sunshine or partial shade**
- **Retentive fertile soil**
- **Summer flowering**

The masterwort *A. major* is a fascinating perennial. Each flowerhead has outer bracts that are stiff, papery and pointed, and in the centre of each individual flower are many tiny florets. The whole umbel presents a number of star-like flowers. The foliage is palmate. The colour of the flowers is a pure rose-pink, with a pinkish collar of the petal-like bracts. The flowers are supported on wiry stems 60cm/2ft high. Other varieties have greenish-white or pale green collars of bracts. One variety, 'Sunningdale Variegated', has leaves prettily splashed with yellow and cream, but as the season advances they lose their variegation unless old flower stems are cut back.

To be successful, astrantias must be in a soil that does not dry out in the summer. To achieve this, a thin dappled or partial shade is an advantage in helping the soil retain moisture.

Propagate by seed sown as soon as it has been gathered, or by division in spring.

Take care
Do not allow these plants to become too dry.

Brunnera macrophylla
(Siberian bugloss)
- **Sunshine or partial shade**
- **Damp soil**
- **Spring flowering**

B. macrophylla, when I first knew this plant, was called *Anchusa myosotidiflora*, the species name indicating that the flowers were similar in appearance to forget-me-nots.

It is one of the first of the border plants to produce blue flowers in spring. The basal leaves are rough, heart-shaped and large, on stalks about 38-45cm/15-18in long, which carry sprays of small blue flowers. In the garden, young plants from self-sown seed can easily be removed and replanted to form a new clump, or given away.

There is also an attractive variegated form, *B. macrophylla* 'Variegata', which has prettily marked creamy-white leaves. The variety needs a sheltered spot, and the soil must not dry out.

Propagate by root cuttings, which are like thick black leather bootlaces or, alternatively, by division in early autumn.

Take care
To prevent self-sown seedlings from taking hold in the garden, remove flowerheads as soon as they have faded.

Right: **Brunnera macrophylla**
Tiny blue flowers appear above the large hairy leaves of this plant during the spring months. It will grow happily in sun or partial shade.

Campanula lactiflora

(Milky bellflower)
● **Full sun**
● **Deep fertile soil**
● **Early to late summer flowering**

This is a superb perennial which will eventually reach a height of 120-150cm/4-5ft, and in partial shade may reach up to180cm/6ft, though it is a better-looking specimen when grown in full sun. Its stout stems require staking in windy gardens. The rootstock, although vigorous, fortunately does not rampage in the soil. The rigid stems carry loose or dense panicles of white or pale blue to deep lilac flowers. The stems are clothed with small light green leaves.

The flesh-pink 'Loddon Anna' is a lovely form of *C. lactiflora*, reaching 120-150cm/4-5ft. The baby of this species 'Pouffe', only 25cm/10in high, is an ideal dwarf plant, with light green foliage forming mounds that are smothered for weeks with lavender-blue flowers during the early and midsummer months.

Propagate this plant by division or by cuttings in the spring.

Take care
These campanulas need moisture during the growing season.

Chelone obliqua

(Balmony, Snakehead, Turtlehead)
● **Sun but tolerates light shade**
● **Fertile well-drained soil**
● **Autumn flowering**

This rather strange-looking perennial derives its popular name from the unusual shape of the flowers. It is a close relation of the penstemons and is sometimes confused with them. Its dark green leaves are broad to oblong in shape, 5-20cm/2-8in long, and arranged in pairs, the last two being just below the erect crowded truss of rosy-purple flowers. The square stems are 60-90cm/2-3ft tall. Provided it is given a sunny position in the border, this plant will produce blooms for several weeks in autumn. The flowers are very weather resistant, which is useful in wet seasons. Its roots have a spreading habit, and plants soon form a mat.

Propagate by seed sown in spring under glass in a temperature of 13-18°C/55-65°F, or in late spring without heat in a cold frame, or by division of roots in spring, or in late autumn as soon as the flowers fade.

Take care
Chelones may invade and crowd out less tough-growing plants.

Chrysanthemum maximum

(Daisy chrysanthemum, Max chrysanthemum, Shasta daisy)
● **Sunny location**
● **Any good fertile soil**
● **Summer flowering**

The Shasta daisy, a native of the Pyrenees, is a must for any perennial border. The height varies from 60-90cm/2-3ft. The flowers are single or double, with plain or fringed petals. On account of the large flat heads, rain and wind can soon knock plants over; short peasticks should be inserted in the ground before the plants become too advanced.

One of the best-known varieties is 'Esther Read', 45cm/18in tall, with pure white, fully double flowers; 'Wirral Pride' is a 90cm/3ft beauty with large anemone-centred blooms; another variety is the fully double white-flowered 'Wirral Supreme', 80cm/32in high. If you prefer a large, fully double frilly-flowered variety, plant 'Droitwich Beauty', 80-90cm/32-36in tall; a creamy-yellow variety is 'Mary Stoker', 80cm/32in high.

Propagate by softwood cuttings in summer, or by division in autumn or spring.

Take care
Be sure to provide support.

Left: **Campanula lactiflora 'Pouffe'**
This charming miniature campanula has little green hummocks covered in lavender-blue flowers. A superb dwarf plant.

Above: **Chelone obliqua**
A perennial with unusually shaped flowers that resemble a turtle's head. Do not grow near weaker plants; it will spread quickly.

Below: **Chrysanthemum maximum**
Every garden should contain a clump of these dependable perennials. They tolerate all soils and are available with single or double blooms.

Cortaderia selloana

(C. argentea)

(Pampas grass)

● **Full sun**
● **Light fertile soil**
● **Late summer and early autumn flowering**

Pampas grass has masses of gracefully arching leaves that forms a good base for the erect stems to carry their silky silvery-white plumes. For indoor decoration gather plumes as soon as they are fully developed.

Varieties include: 'Monstrosa', creamy-white plumes, 2.75m/9ft stems; compact 'Pumila', with short foliage, creamy-white plumes, erect 1.5m/5ft stems; 'Sunningdale Silver', creamy-white open plumes, 2.1m/7ft stems; 'Rendatleri', silver-pink plumes, 1.8-2.1m/6-8ft stems.

They are not fussy over soil but are happiest in light soils enriched with humus or well-rotted farmyard manure or good garden compost, which will retain moisture. Plant in either autumn or spring. Winter care entails allowing the grass to die down. Never cut it with shears; wear stout leather gloves to pull the leaves out of established clumps.

Propagate by seed under glass in spring, or by division in spring.

Take care
Give ample moisture during very hot weather.

Right: **Cortaderia selloana 'Pumila'**
This splendid compact variety of pampas grass produces creamy-white plumes during late summer to early autumn.

Above: **Crocosmia masonorum**
A fully hardy perennial, it can be shy to flower initially but after a few years it will provide a good show of colour. Suitable for sandy soil.

Crocosmia masonorum
(Montbretia, Montebretia)
● Sun or partial shade
● Light, fertile and well-drained soil
● Summer flowering

C. masonorum is a rather special montbretia. There are two main differences between this one and *C. x crocosmiflora*: the striking ribbed strap-like foliages is broader in *C. masonorum* and the the intense flame-orange flowers are carried on top of the arching stems, instead of being arranged beneath the stems as in *C. x crocosmia*.

When this crocosmia became popular around 1953, it was considered not to be fully hardy. However, its survival through some severe winters has proved otherwise.

The corms are small, and the first year after planting they are shy to flower, but planted 15cm/6in apart and left alone for three or four years, they will soon create a splendid clump. Divide corms in early spring.

Take care
Do not attempt to lift and replant while the corms are doing well.

Echinacea purpurea
(Purple cone flower)
● Sunny location
● Well-drained soil
● Summer flowering

For many years this strongly-growing perennial was known as *Rudbeckia purpurea*. It is a stately plant with dark green foliage, rough to the touch, on stiff stout stems. The rich reddish-purple flowers have a central boss of orange-brown which makes them quite outstanding. Over the years there have been many varieties raised. The variety I remember when first working in a nursery was called 'The King', 1.2m/4ft tall, and it is still available. An earlier flowering variety is the broad-petalled erect carmine-purple flowered 'Robert Bloom', which is 90cm/3ft tall. If you want a variety of colours, the Bressingham Hybrids, also 90cm/3ft tall, are well worth planting.

The echinaceas are best planted in spring. Add leaf-mould or compost to the soil at the time of planting. Propagate by seed sown in spring, by root cuttings in autumn, or by division in spring.

Take care
Choose a sunny spot.

Left: **Echinacea purpurea**
This hardy perennial is a stately plant, its richly coloured flowers appearing in midsummer. It is a strongly-growing subject that will thrive in sunshine and warmth.

47

Above: **Eupatorium purpureum
'Atropurpureum'**
*The purplish foliage of this pretty variety is an
added bonus to the autumnal rose-lilac flowers.
Eminently suitable for a wild garden.*

Eupatorium purpureum 'Atropurpureum'

*(Joe-pye weed, Purple hemp agrimony,
Trumpet weed)*
- **Sunny location**
- **Any good fertile soil**
- **Early autumn flowering**

This plant has always attracted my attention by
its tall handsome upright purplish stems,
bedecked with large fluffy branching heads of
flowers in varying shades of pale purple, mauve-
pink, cinnamon-pink, purplish-rose, and purple-
lilac. My reason for giving such a list of colours is
that much depends on the individual admirer of
this 1.5-1.8m/5-6ft dominating perennial. The
variety 'Atropurpureum' has foliage that is
purplish and its fluffy flowers are rosy-lilac.

In a large border it needs to be planted well
behind shorter-growing plants, or they will be
hidden. This North American plant needs good
rich soil; a mulch in spring with manure or good
garden compost will be welcome. This is an ideal
perennial to grow in a wild or semi-wild garden.
Propagation by division in autumn.

Take care
Make sure plants are not starved.

Filipendula purpurea

(Spiraea palmatum)
(Dropwort, Meadowsweet)
- **Sun or partial shade**
- **Cool moist conditions**
- **Summer flowering**

This Japanese hardy herbaceous perennial is
one of half a dozen dropworts. It can still be
found in some nursery catalogues and garden
centres under its old name, *Spiraea palmatum*.
This is a most handsome plant, and if it has most
soil or is growing near the side of a pond, it will
not fail to attract attention. It has large, lobed
leaves and above the elegant leafy crimson
stems are large flat heads bearing many tiny
carmine-rose flowers, each stem reaching a
height of 60-120cm/2-4ft. The pinkish *F. rubra*
has large flowerheads up to 28cm/11in across. In
damp soil it will form huge clumps, in either sun
or shade.

To obtain the best results, grow this plant in
partial shade and in rich fertile moist soil.
Propagate by seeds sown in pans or boxes
under glass in autumn, or by division in autumn.

Take care
Make sure that this plant does not lack moisture.

Right: **Filipendula purpurea**
*A splendid plant for a cool spot. The handsome
foliage is crowned with lovely carmine-rose
flowers on stems 60-120cm/2-4ft high.*

Galega officinalis
(Goat's rue)

- Full sun
- Any good soil, or even poor soils
- Summer flowering

This is a perennial that needs to be at the back of the border, as it has a rather sprawling habit, so plant it behind perennials that can shield it when the flowers have faded and the plant is looking a little the worse for wear. What a joy goat's rue is, as it will thrive in any sunny corner and in any good soil. The small pea-shaped flowers of *G. officinalis* are mauve, and they are borne on branching stems up to 1.5m/5ft tall. As a contrast to *G. officinalis* there is an attractive white variety called 'Candida'.

Plant in the autumn or during the early spring and allow sufficient room for each specimen to develop. They will thrive particularly well in a sunny location and are generally free of most pests and diseases.

Propagate by division in autumn or spring.

Take care
Insert a few peasticks in the ground early in the year. The plants will eventually grow through to hide them.

Above: **Galega officinalis**
Galegas have a sprawling habit and are best planted near the back of the border. Small pea-shaped blooms are borne on branching stems.

49

Galtonia candicans

(Hyancinthus candicans)

(Summer hyacinth)

- Full sun
- Deep fertile soil
- Late summer flowering

This hardy bulbous plant has fragrant white dangling bell-like flowers carried on 90-120cm/ 3-4ft stout tube-like stems; at the base are long glaucous-green leaves.

This bulb has to be planted 15cm/6in below the soil, which needs to be well drained. Bulbs can be planted in autumn or spring, and in a year or so they will be established. If they are planted behind the violet-flowered liriope, the two may flower together. This bulb needs good fertile soil, as bulbs may deteriorate in poor sandy soil. Once established they should be left undisturbed. Propagate by detaching offsets in spring, but not too often. Seeds can be sown as soon as ripe out of doors, or under glass in spring. Galtonia will readily produce quantities of self-sown seedlings.

Take care
Add plenty of humus, such as well-rotted farmyard manure or well-rotted garden compost, before planting bulbs.

Above: **Galtonia candicans**
Once established, this bulbous plant will produce fragrant white blooms in late summer. Plant the bulbs 15cm/6in deep in fertile soil.

Hemerocallis

(Day lily)

- Sun or partial shade
- Any soil but avoid dry ones
- Summer flowering

The day lilies are hardy, the large clumps producing an abundance of bright green arching foliage and a display of scented lily-like flowers over a long period. The flowers of early day lilies lasted for only one day, but modern varieties last two or sometimes three days. The lily-like flowers are carried at the top of stout 90cm/3ft stems.

Three modern varieties are: 'Pink Damask', with pretty pink flowers, 75cm/30in; 'Nashville', large, creamy-yellow with streaked orange-red throat markings, 90cm/3ft; and the glowing bright red 'Stafford', 75cm/30in.

Propagate day lilies by division in spring. Plants can be left undisturbed for many years; lift and divide them only when clumps become overcrowded.

Take care
In very hot dry weather, give these plants a thorough soaking.

Right: **Hemerocallis 'Pink Damask'**
The beautiful pink lily-like blooms of this recommended variety are carried on stems up to 75cm/30in in height. Allow these superb plants to grow undisturbed in good soil.

Heuchera pulchella 'Red Spangles'

(Alum root, Coral bells, Coral flower)
- Sun or partial shade
- Well-drained fertile soil
- Early summer flowering

Heucheras have evergreen heart-shaped leaves and their pretty tiny bell-shaped flowers hang down from slender wiry stems. The foliage comes in various shades of green, sometimes with zonal markings marbled like pelargoniums. 'Red Spangles' has crimson-scarlet flowers and is 50cm/20in tall.

Heucheras make bold clumps as much as 30cm/1ft wide, but deteriorate if not divided and transplanted every few years; throw out woody pieces, keeping only the young vigorous ones. Work in well-rotted garden compost or well-rotted manure before planting. Heucheras prefer a light, well-drained fertile soil, but dislike cold clay, wet or very acid soils. Given good feeding, flowers will be produced from spring to early autumn. Propagate by division in late summer or early autumn.

Take care
Keep moist during hot days in the summer.

Right: **Heuchera pulchella 'Red Spangles'**
This is one of the best varieties to grow; its blood-red bell-shaped flowers are borne on slender stems up to 50cm/20in in height.

Liatris spicata 'Kobold'

(Blazing star, Gay feather, Spike gayfeather)

● **Full sun**
● **Ordinary well-drained soil**
● **Summer flowering**

The flowers of liatris open at the top first, whereas most plants that have spike-like flowers open from the base, and those at the top open last. The small strap-like leaves form a rosette near the ground; the flower stems also have small leaves. The flowerheads are closely packed and look not unlike a paint brush. The variety 'Kobold' has brilliant pinky-mauve flowers, 60cm/2ft tall. Also recommended is *L. pycnostachya*, the Kansas feather, with pinky-purple crowded flowerheads, 15-20cm/6-8in long, on rather floppy 1.2m/4ft stems. It makes a fine display in late summer and early autumn. Liatris are useful as cut flowers and ideal for drying for winter flower arrangements.

The species is better in poor soil, and prefers firm ground. Propagate by seed sown in pans in early spring, or by division in late spring.

Take care
Do not grow in rich soil.

Left: **Liatris spicata 'Kobold'**
The frothy flowers have the unusual habit of opening from the top downwards. This lovely variety has pink-purple flower spikes that can be cut for indoor arrangements.

Liriope muscari
(Big blue liriopes, Turf lily)
- Sunny location
- Fertile soil with moderate drainage
- Late summer or autumn flowering

As its name suggests, *L. muscari* is not unlike an outsize grape hyacinth. Its foliage arches over, forming a neat hummock from which the 23-30cm/9-12in stems arise, bearing lilac-mauve flowers crowded together and looking rather like a bottle brush. I have seen liriope used most effectively as an edging to a border of shrubs; it is always useful to have a few of these evergreen plants in a border during winter.

Having grown liriope in a clay soil with a pH 6.5 reading, which is an almost neutral soil, I went on to grow it in a light acid soil with a pH of 5 to 5.5, and the plant in the light acid soil looked very much happier. In my experience, this tuberous-rooted plant does better in full sun than in shade or partial shade. Propagate it by division in spring.

Take care
Give these plants a sunny spot in which to grow.

Lobelia cardinalis
(Cardinal flower)
- Sunny location
- Rich, fertile and moist soil
- Late summer flowering

The cardinal flower is one of the most handsome herbaceous perennials. Above a rosette of green leaves, which also cover the stem, are brilliant scarlet blooms. The stems are 90cm/3ft high.

Planting is best done in spring; initial preparation is essential, and plenty of moistened peat, leaf-mould or well-rotted garden compost should be incorporated. This species likes rich moist soil. If the ground is not forked over or cleaned for the winter, plants will come through unscathed in areas that are more or less frost-free; if doubtful, lift them in autumn and store in a dry frost-proof shed, covering the roots with peat or leaf-mould. Propagate by division in spring when the plants can be taken out of store.

Take care
Never let the roots suffer from drought during the growing season, and ensure that they have adequate moisture.

Above: **Lobelia 'Brightness'**
This is one of the best of the many hybrids. Its bright scarlet flowers appear in late summer on stems up to 90cm/3ft tall.

Left: **Liriope muscari**
A hardy evergreen perennial with arching grass-like foliage that forms a neat hummock in the border. In late summer and autumn erect stems of lilac-mauve blooms appear.

Lychnis coronaria 'Abbotswood Rose'

(Agrostemma coronaria)

(Campion, Catchfly, Mullein pink)

- ● **Full sun**
- ● **Fertile well-drained soil**
- ● **Summer flowering**

This short-lived hardy herbaceous perennial has attractive soft furry foliage; its leaves are coated with fine silver hairs, which almost cover the entire plant. The leaves are borne in pairs from a basal clump up the 60cm/2ft stems on which the branching sprays of dianthus-like brilliant rose-crimson flowers of 'Abbotswood Rose' are carried (some call the flowers rose-pink). It is a lovely plant, and a clump of five plants to a square metre/square yard will add charm and colour to any perennial border.

There is also a variety 'Alba', which has white flowers; apart from the colour, it is similar to the variety 'Abbotswood Rose'.

Propagate by division in autumn, but if the soil is cold and wet, leave it until spring.

Take care

These plants need a fertile soil.

Above: **Lychnis coronaria 'Abbotswood Rose'**
Branching sprays of rose-crimson flowers adorn this plant during the summer. The silvery foliage is an excellent foil to the blooms.

Right: **Macleaya microcarpa**
An imposing perennial that should be given ample room to spread. The plumes of flowers reach 2.4m/8ft in late summer.

Macleaya cordata
(Plume poppy)
- **Sun or light shade**
- **Rich fertile soil**
- **Late summer flowering**

This impressive and dramatic-looking hardy herbaceous perennial may grow to 2.1m/7ft tall. The rough, fig-like, palm-shaped, sculptured, glaucous foliage, silver beneath, forms a dominating clump from which stiff tall stems arise displaying the small panicles of yellow plume-like fluffy flowers without petals. It is a plant for an isolated bed or at the back of a large border, for if too near the front it will obscure any plants behind it. For a slightly earlier display of flesh-tinted buff flowers grow the similar *M. microcarpa*.

The plume poppy has wandering roots but this should not put anyone off; if you can find a suitable part of the border or garden, it is well worth growing. Plant in spring. Propagate by half-ripe cuttings in early summer, by suckers or root cuttings in autumn, or by division in spring.

Take care
Choose the ideal position for this dramatic plant.

Above: **Oenothera missouriensis**
A superb ground cover plant with dark green narrow leaves that hug the ground and red-spotted bright yellow flowers borne on red stems. It must have a freely draining soil in order to succeed.

Oenothera missouriensis
(Evening primrose)
- **Sunny location**
- **Well-drained soil**
- **Summer and autumn flowering**

This lovely perennial ground-hugging plant, which belongs to the evening primrose family, is a native of the southern United States of America. The dark green narrow leaves lie prostrate on the ground, and above them are produced canary-yellow flowers about 7.5cm/3in across, on 23cm/9in reddish stems, in succession for many weeks during the summer. The flowers, which open in the evening and last for several days, are followed by equally large seedpods. Often the buds are spotted with red.

This is a superb plant for the front of a border, but to succeed it must have a well-drained soil. It is ideal for the rock garden but allow it sufficient space, because it can spread up to 60cm/2ft. Propagate this species by seed in spring.

Take care
Choose a well-drained soil.

Phlox paniculata

(P. decussata)

(Border phlox, Perennial phlox,
Summer perennial phlox)

● **Sun or light shade**
● **Light fertile soil**
● **Summer to late summer flowering**

This hardy herbaceous perennial is a well-known
garden plant, also called *Phlox decussata*. It
develops 15cm/6in long, terminal, tapering heads
of flowers each up to 2.5cm/1in wide from
midsummer to late summer.

Many older varieties are no longer easily
available, but there is still a good selection of
varieties and colours. The purple-red 'Vintage
Wine' (above left) has huge trusses, on
75cm/30in stems; 'Windsor' (above right) is clear
carmine with a magenta eye, 1.1m/44in tall; the
strong 'Border Gem' is cyclamen-purple with a
peony-purple eye, 90cm/3ft tall; 'Mother of Pearl'
has pretty pink trusses and is 75cm/30in tall; the
dark-foliaged blue 'Hampton Court' is of similar

height; and for a variegated variety there is
'Harlequin' bearing rich purple flowers, 90cm/3ft
tall. 'Prince of Orange' is a stunning orange-
salmon colour, also 90cm/3ft high; the pure white
Fujuyana from the USA has magnificent
cylindrical trusses and is 75cm/30in tall; two
90cm/3ft beauties are the pale lilac 'Prospero'
and the deep crimson 'Red Indian'. For a pure
white choose 'White Admiral', 75cm/30in high.

Phlox are best in a light soil with a good supply
of humus, well-rotted farmyard manure or
well-rotted garden compost, and – in very dry
weather – sufficient moisture for their needs.
What they do not like is chalk or clay soils. Gritty
or gravelly soils are satisfactory, provided there is
enough humus and the soil is never allowed to
dry out completely.

Only one pest attacks phlox: that is the
eelworm. To avoid it, propagate plants from root
cuttings in autumn or winter.

Take care
Do not let phlox dry out in very hot dry summers.

Above: **Physostegia virginiana 'Rose Bouquet'**
Spires of tubular pink-mauve flowers up to
60cm/2ft long are carried above the large,
coarsely-toothed leaves during the late summer.

Above: **Phlox paniculata 'Vintage Wine'**
This purple-red variety has fairly compact flower
trusses that are freely produced on stems
75cm/30in tall. Beautifully fragrant.

Above: **Phlox paniculata 'Windsor'**
One of the taller varieties, this has clear carmine
flowers, each with a magenta eye, and grows to
over 1m/39in in height.

Physostegia virginiana
(Obedience, Obedient plant)
- Sun or partial shade
- Any good fertile soil
- Late summer flowering

This hardy herbaceous perennial is well named the obedient plant because its flowers have hinged stalks and can be moved from side to side and remain as altered on their square stems. The long and narrow glossy dark green leaves are toothed and grow in four columns; the dull rose-pink flowers terminate the square tapering spikes, 45-105cm/18-42in tall. They bloom from summer to autumn, until the frosts spoil their beauty. Physostegia has vigorous stoloniferous rootstocks that spread underground.

There are several good varieties: 'Rose Bouquet' has pinkish-mauve trumpet flowers; 'Summer Snow', pure white, is about 75cm/30in high; and 'Vivid' bears rose-crimson flowers on stalks 30-45cm/12-18in tall.

Propagate by division in spring, or by root cuttings in winter.

Take care
Provide sufficient moisture during dry weather.

Potentilla gelida
(P. atrosanguinea)
(Cinquefoil)
- Full sun
- Fertile well-drained soil
- Early and late summer flowering

The best-known variety of potentilla is 'Gibson's Scarlet', which has brilliant single red flowers on 30cm/1ft stems from mid- to late summer. Larger-flowered varieties include the double orange-flame 'William Rollison', also the double mahogany-coloured 'Monsieur Rouillard'; and the grey-foliaged 'Gloire de Nancy', which has semi-double orange-crimson flowers almost 5cm/2in across, on 45cm/18in branching stems; all bloom from early to late summer.

The potentillas, with strawberry-like foliage, are best in full sun, but can tolerate partial shade. They enjoy good well-drained soil, but if the soil is too rich it results in extra lush foliage at the expense of the flowers. Avoid growing potentillas in moist or stagnant ground in winter.

Propagate by division in spring or autumn.

Take care
These potentillas sprawl, so give them ample space; plant in groups.

Left: **Potentilla gelida 'Gibson's Scarlet'**
Stunning single red flowers are produced on 30cm/1ft stems above strawberry-like foliage from mid- to late summer.

57

Rudbeckia fulgida
(Rudbeckia newmanii, Rudbeckia speciosa)
(Black-eyed Susan, Coneflower)
- **Full sun**
- **Moist fertile soil**
- **Late summer and autumn flowering**

This species has also been known as *R. speciosa* and *R. newmanii*, but whatever one calls it, it is one of the most useful border and cut flowers in late summer and autumn. Erect 60cm/2ft stems rise from leafy clumps, displaying several large golden-yellow daisy-like flowers with short blackish-purple central discs or cones, hence the name 'black-eyed Susan'. The narrow leaves are rather rough to handle.

Other garden forms of *R. fulgida* are the free-flowering *R. deamii*, 90cm/3ft tall, and 'Goldsturm', which above its bushy growth has stems 60cm/2ft tall carrying chrome-yellow flowers with dark brown cones. Rudbeckias make good cut flowers and blend very well with *Aster amellus* 'King George'.

Propagate by dividing the plants during the autumn or spring.

Take care
Do not let these dry out during the summer.

Left: **Rudbeckia fulgida 'Goldsturm'**
These bright yellow flowers with dark brown cones are superb for cutting from late summer through into the autumn.

Above: **Saponaria officinalis**
This is the original single-flowered form, with fragrant rose-pink blooms. Double-flowered forms are also available.

Saponaria officinalis
(Bouncing bet, Soapwort)
● Sunny location
● Well-drained soil
● Summer to early autumn flowering

This plant is called soapwort because a lather can be made from the foliage and used for cleaning old curtains. This wilding can be seen in hedgerows in summer and early autumn. It is a handsome perennial, but its roots can spread beneath the ground. It has panicles of large fragrant rose pink flowers, 2.5-3cm/1-1.2in across, carried on terminal loose heads on erect 60-90cm/2-3ft stems. The three-veined leaves are 5-13cm/2-5in long and 5cm/2in wide.

Double forms are 'Roseo Plena', which is pink, and the white 'Albo Plena'. All do well in good well-drained soil, but lime or chalk soils should be avoided.

Propagate this plant by half-ripe cuttings in summer, or by division in spring.

Take care
These plants can spread and become untidy, but do not exclude them from your garden on this account.

Schizostylis coccinea
(Crimson flag)
● Full sun
● Any moist fertile soil
● Early autumn flowering

Originating in South Africa, this relative of the irises appears to grow and flower freely in most soils. In South Africa it grows near water, and it needs ample moisture to flower. It has long stems, 60-75cm/24-30in or more and its pretty cup-shaped flowers open in a star-like fashion, not unlike small gladiolus flowers. *S. coccinea* has rich crimson blooms about 4cm/1.6in across; 'Major' and 'Gigantea' are even brighter and larger; 'Mrs Hegarty' is pale pink; 'Sunrise' has large pink flowers. The flowering stems are excellent for cutting.

The roots need to be lifted, divided and replanted every few years to keep them thriving. A spring mulch of peat or well-rotted compost will help to retain moisture around the plants. Propagate by division in spring, always leaving four to six shoots on each portion.

Take care
Be sure to keep these plants moist.

Left: **Schizostylis coccinea 'Major'**
In warm moist surroundings this plant will thrive in most types of soil and produce these stunning star-shaped flowers in autumn.

Solidago 'Goldenmosa'

(Aaron's rod, Golden rod)

- **Sun or partial shade**
- **Good ordinary soil**
- **Late summer flowering**

Golden rod, at one time, meant some small yellow one-sided sprays at the top of tall stout hairy stems. Today, there is a much larger selection. The variety 'Goldenmosa' has pretty frothy flowers, miniature heads of the original golden rod, similar to mimosa; the rough hairy flower spikes are 75cm/30in tall. Two smaller varieties are the 45cm/18in 'Cloth of Gold', with deep yellow flowers, and 'Golden Thumb', with clear yellow flowers on 30cm/1ft stems, which produces neat little bushes ideal for the front of the garden border.

These vigorous plants will thrive in any good soil provided it is well supplied with nutrients. A sunny location or one in partial shade will suit them equally well. Propagate them all by division during the spring.

Take care

Apply humus to taller varieties.

Above: **Solidago 'Goldenmosa'**
This superb variety grows to about 75cm/30in in height with lovely frothy yellow flowers. It will grow vigorously in sun or partial shade.

Below: **Tradescantia** x **andersoniana 'Isis'**
The striking deep purple-blue flowers are long-lasting in summer. Plant in clumps for the maximum effect.

Tradescantia x andersoniana 'Isis'

(T. virginiana)

(Spiderwort, Trinity, Widow's tears)

● Sun or partial shade
● Any good fertile soil
● Summer and autumn flowering

The spiderworts are probably better known as houseplants, but the hardy herbaceous perennials are much larger. There are a number of varieties from which to choose. These perennials have smooth, almost glossy, curving strap-shaped leaves, ending in a cradle-like effect, where a continuous display of three-petalled flowers emerges throughout the summer and autumn.

The variety 'Isis' has deep blue flowers and is 45cm/18in high. The pure white 'Osprey', has three-petalled crested flowers, and another pure white of similar height is 'Innocence'. Two 50cm/20in varieties are the carmine-purple 'Purewell Giant' and the rich velvety 'Purple Dome'.

Plant them in clumps, not singly; on their own they are not effective, but clumps make a splash of colour. Propagate them by division in the spring or autumn.

Take care
Plant near the front of a border.

Tropaeolum speciosum

(Flame creeper, Scotch flame flower)

● Shade and sun
● Moisture retentive soil
● Summer and autumn flowering

This beautiful perennial plant can be bitterly disappointing, because its fleshy roots are difficult to establish. Once settled, however, it is a delight. Pretty six-lobed leaves are carried on twining stems that are best seen rambling over evergreen shrubs or hedges. From the midsummer period through to the autumn the plant is covered with a crop of superb scarlet flowers about 4cm/1.6in across and with attractive spurs. The plant is best suited to cool moist country gardens; it is not ideal for growing in towns and cities.

The warm ochre yellow flowers of *T. polyphyllum* are equally lovely, but it prefers its fleshy roots in well-drained hot sunny positions. Propagate by seed sown in spring in a cold frame, or by division in spring.

Take care
Be patient.

Below: **Tropaeolum speciosum**
Bright scarlet flowers appear on the twining stems of this attractive plant throughout the summer. An excellent subject for growing over an evergreen shrub.

Part Three: Bulbs

Introduction

What exactly are bulbs, corms, rhizomes and tubers; what have they in common; and why are they different?

All these root forms are food storage systems built up in one season when the weather allows nutrients to be readily available to them, and then used during the following season when the plants need to grow rapidly and flower during a period when drought, frozen soil or other poor growing conditions occur.

A *bulb* is a collection of old leaf bases around an embryo bud and new leaves that will emerge the next season. A *corm* is the thickened end of a stem that will shoot up and produce leaves along its length. A *rhizome* is a horizontal stem – sometimes above ground and at other times below the surface – which will sprout tufts of leaves; sometimes it runs under the ground and emerges some distance from the parent plant. A *tuber* is a swollen root that stores goodness for the coming year.

Most of these plants produce underground offshoots that can be removed and grown on separately to become mature plants. Bulbs often produce smaller bulbs around the root area, called *bulblets*, which can be separated and replanted in protected nursery beds. Corms produce a new corm either above or next to the original one, and often smaller ones are also produced, which can be treated in the same way as bulblets to reach full maturity. Rhizomes and tubers are usually divided by cutting but each piece must have an eye or small shoot to grow; if there is a root system as well, each section must have some rooting growth in order to survive.

Buying bulbs

There are many places for buying bulbs – garden centres, nurseries, supermarkets and mail order specialists – and it is quite a simple matter to find what you are looking for; but do be wary of cheap offers, for in this field you get only what you pay for, and other people's rejects are often disposed of in this way. It is better to buy one good bulb than a dozen poor ones.

Bulbs come in different sizes and forms. In the narcissus family there are 'mother' bulbs, which will produce a number of shoots and flowers, and can then be divided up to give several individual bulbs. 'Double nose' bulbs should give two shoots and flowers. Offsets are unlikely to be mature enough to flower in the first year. Some suppliers give quantity discounts, and these should be treated as genuine bargains and not confused with cheap offers. Bruised or damaged bulbs, or specimens that show any signs of insect attack or mould, should be avoided wherever possible. Spare bulbs from friends or neighbours may carry disease and pests; if you plan to use them, give the bulbs and the surrounding soil a liberal dose of pesticide and fungicide as a precaution.

Storing bulbs

At the end of the growing season it is sometimes necessary to lift and store bulbs. They should be sorted, named and treated with a fungicide. Some will need to be covered with moist peat, but others will require a dry covering. Keep them in a cool place that is frost-free, not too dry (or the bulbs will shrivel) and ensure they are protected against marauding pests such as mice. Inspect your store of bulbs during the winter and remove any that

are beginning to rot or show disease. Tubers that are drying out and look shrivelled can be soaked in water overnight, then dried on the surface and replaced in store. By taking care during the winter months you should have healthy bulbs to plant when the season is right.

Health

To keep disease and pest attack to a minimum it is best to prevent trouble before it starts, by treating the plant and the surrounding soil with an appropriate preparation. This can be a chemical, but for those who have deep feelings against chemicals there are natural products that will help to fend off any attack. Whether they are man-made or natural, treat every such product with a measure of respect, and always keep to the manufacturer's instructions. A solution may look a little weak, but resist the temptation to make it stronger; it is when we fail to use the right dose that trouble starts. As a general rule, a good healthy plant will keep disease at bay and shrug off a few pests; it is the weaker plants that attract trouble and spread it to the rest of the garden.

Planting

Before planting takes place, a little preparation is important. First, plan where the bulbs are to be placed, how many, and in what shape or order. Once this is decided, then the area of soil can be

Below: **Dahlia 'Gypsy Dance'**
These grow best in a medium to heavy soil and need an open, sunny position. They are ideal as bedding subjects and do not require staking. Water well in hot weather.

Above: **Four types of food storage** (from left): Bulb – leaf storage; corm – stem supply; rhizome – swollen stem; tuber – enlarged root.

prepared and dug over, all weed roots removed and drainage supplied if necessary: often a good dose of bulky manure, sharp sand or leaf-mould is sufficient to open the texture of the soil and improve the drainage. Peat can be added where there is a need for more moisture; this, together with manure and leaf-mould, can be either dug well in or left as a thick layer of mulch on the surface, but do take care that manure is not in direct contact with the bulb and that the manure used is old and well rotted. Where the soil is particularly boggy, a series of land drains should be laid in order to drain the soil. If this proves impossible, it is better to use the land to good advantage, and make a bog garden planted with moisture-loving specimens.

Feeding

It is important to provide food each season, so that every plant will have built up strength to produce leaves and flowers during the next growth period. In most cases, feeding takes place either when the leaves are mature and can absorb nourishment even if the flowers have finished blooming, or – in the case of the colchicum – before the flowers appear. A surface dressing of a general fertilizer will be washed into the soil by the rain and taken up by the roots. A mulch of compost will follow the same path with the added advantage of supplying humus to improve the soil. A good dose of liquid manure will feed the plants through its leaves as well as through its roots. All these types of feed will do wonders to the plant, fattening up the roots and storage growths for the next year, when the size and blooms will be much improved. Watering is important, too; make sure that the bulb is kept moist during the feeding period. If drought occurs, check that the soil has not dried out, and if it has, give a copious draught so that the soil is thoroughly soaked down to the bulb roots. A mere sprinkle of water will just dampen the surface and simply encourage the roots to grow towards the moisture, which will quickly dry out.

Propagation

In general, the increase of plants occurs naturally through seed, by increase of roots, or by layering (stems touch the soil and develop a new root system, and gradually become independent). In most cases bulbs produce small bulblets around the parent bulb, which grow into full-sized ones in a year or two; these should replace other bulbs that are lost through age, disease, drought, pests or poor conditions. Plants grown from seed will in some cases take six years or more to reach the flowering stage, and for most of us this is far too long to wait – even waiting for bulblets to produce blooms is sometimes more than we can bear, so we have to resort to buying bulbs to give us instant gardens. Even if we purchase bulbs, however, we can still keep a small bed of bulblets or even a pot in a sheltered part of the garden. To keep the young plants from being choked with weeds, grow them in a sterilized potting mixture. This will give them a balanced soil to grow in, a good start in life, and a better chance to reach maturity. Where seed is recommended for increasing stock, a seed-growing mixture should be used and the instructions given in the text of this section should be followed.

Indoor forcing

To provide blooms out of season or even a few weeks earlier the bulb growers have devised a system of cultivation which utilizes both cold and warm storage, in order that spring flowers are available during the winter months. Plant them in containers of peat and charcoal, provide them with moisture, and keep them in the dark to sprout. When the shoot has emerged from the bulb and grown to the desired length bring the plants out into the light and warmth, where they will bloom. After flowering they can be planted out in the garden, but some bulbs take a long time to recover their natural cycle. Many bulbs which are suitable for cultivating and growing indoors can now be purchased complete with pot and soil.

Selection

The plants featured have been selected to give a broad range of different types, and most are readily available commercially. They include hardy, half-hardy and tender forms. Hardy plants will survive in the colder regions of the temperate zone, and can withstand prolonged frost and moderately hot weather. Half-hardy ones are from warmer regions of the temperate area, stand up to the occasional frost, and thrive in heat. Tender types are best kept to areas where there is little frost or where protection can be given. In the case of dormant bulbs, a thick layer of straw, compost, bracken or peat will insulate them. In colder areas it is best to treat the tender plants as pot specimens to be kept in the greenhouse or indoors. The choice of plants in this section gives a variety of flower, leaf and size; you should be able to find plants that you can fit into existing schemes without having to alter the planting to see the new varieties. There are small subjects suitable for the alpine garden as well as for the border, larger subjects for the back of the herbaceous border, and medium ones that can stand alone or mix with other plants. Whichever sort you choose you can have flowers the whole year round provided you pick the right varieties.

Names given are, in most cases, the Latin ones that are known in all countries; the common names can vary from district to district. The most common names are given after the Latin name to help identification. The planting depths indicate the recommended distance between the top of the bulb and the soil surface.

David Papworth

A-Z Index by Latin Name

Above: **Alstroemeria aurantiaca**
The rich colour and exotic markings of this plant contrast with the blue-grey leaves in summer. Place it in a sheltered site in full sun.

Alstroemeria aurantiaca
(Lily-of-the-Incas, Peruvian lily)
● **Sunny and sheltered site**
● **Well-drained fertile soil**
● **Plant tubers 10-15cm/4-6in deep**

This tuberous-rooted plant has twisted blue-grey leaves, and grows to a height of 90cm/3ft. Borne on leafy stems, the flowers are a distinctive trumpet-shape in orange-reds, the upper two petals having red veins.

Plant the tubers in spring. Cover with a mulch of compost or well-rotted manure in spring. As they grow, support to prevent them being blown over. Dead-head plants to encourage more blooms. In autumn cut stems down to the ground. In spring the plants can be divided, but take care not to disturb the roots unduly. Sometimes the plant will not produce any stems, leaves or flowers during the first season, but once established it can be left for years. Sow the seed in the spring in a cold frame, and plant out into the garden a year later.

Watch for slugs and caterpillars, and use a suitable insecticide if necessary. When the plant shows yellow mottling and distorted growth, destroy it – this is a virus disease.

Take care
Avoid damaging the roots.

Anemone blanda
(Blue windflower)
● **Sun or light shade**
● **Well-drained soil**
● **Plant 5cm/2in deep**

This spring-flowering plant grows to 15cm/6in tall; the daisy-like flowers, in white, pink, red-tipped, lavender or pale blue, and 3.5cm/1.4in across, appear during the spring. They make an ideal rockery plant and can be grown in clumps under trees.

Anemones tolerate either alkaline or acid soils provided they are well-drained. Corms should be planted 10cm/4in apart in the autumn. Lift the corms after the leaves have died down in early autumn; divide, and remove offsets for replanting. Sow the seeds in the late summer, and germinate them in a cold frame; transplant the seedlings, and grow them on for two years before moving them out to their final growing positions in the garden.

If plant and soil are treated with a general insecticide you should have little trouble. Stunted yellow leaves and meagre flowers indicate a virus attack; destroy plants before the virus has a chance to spread.

Take care
Soak corms for 48 hours before planting.

Right: **Anemone blanda 'Blue Pearl'**
This fine low-growing plant brightens up the border and rock garden in late winter and early spring with its finely-shaped blooms. It forms a clump and will grow happily in either sun or shade and in a well-drained soil.

Begonia x tuberhybrida

(Tuberous begonia)
- Slight shade
- Humid atmosphere and moist soil
- Plant flush with the soil

The parents of this tuberous-rooted group come from China, Japan and Socotra, an island in the Indian Ocean. The plants form a very popular series of hybrids or crosses with large rose-like flowers and mid-green ear-shaped leaves. The plants grow to 60cm/2ft tall, with a spread of 45cm/18in. Both male and female flowers are borne on the same plant: the females are single blooms, but the males are more noticeable, being double in form and 7.5-15cm/3-6in across. They flower from summer to late autumn, and are very popular as both bedding and pot plants. The range of colours is wide, with brilliant hues of yellow, orange, reds, pink and white; some have bands of red edging to the petals and are known as picotee begonias.

The tubers are started in damp peat when a temperature of 16°C/60°F can be kept, the tubers being placed just level with the surface and with the flat or slightly hollow surface uppermost. As the leaves start shooting, the tuber should be lifted and put into a pot with a moist growing medium. As the roots fill the pot, move to a larger container and support the stems with a cane. Once established the pots should be given an occasional liquid feed. At the end of spring the danger of frost should have passed and they can then safely be planted out in the open.

To retain deep colours, keep the plant out of direct sunshine and prevent overheating by spraying it with water. Larger flowers can be produced by removing the single female blooms and allowing only one shoot to each tuber; remove the other shoots and use them as cuttings. Push these into a sharp soil and keep moist until rooted. Sow seeds in winter at the same temperature as when tubers are started and you should get flowers the same year; tubers will be formed and they can be kept for the following year. At the end of the growing season, when the leaves start to turn yellow or the first frost occurs, the plants can be lifted and kept in a frost-free place until they have died back. The tubers can be separated from the dead leaves and stem, and stored in peat where

there is protection from frost through the winter until the following year, when they can be started off again on their next cycle.

Pendent varieties are ideal for hanging baskets, containers and windowboxes where they can spill over the edge. The winter flowering Lorraine begonias are grown in spring from cuttings and should be kept at 10°C/50°F for the flowers to continue throughout the winter. These plants should be kept just moist. When growing from seed, mix the seeds with some fine sand, spread the mixture over the surface of the seed-growing medium, press down and put no additional soil on top; this will even the distribution of the seeds. Begonias can also be propagated by dividing the tubers, or by leaf cuttings. Keep pests at bay with a general pesticide; diseases are due to over-wet conditions so use a fungicide too.

Above: **Begonia** x **tuberhybrida**
The rich colour of the large blooms stands out against the dark green leaves. Flowers will appear from early summer to late autumn.

Below: **Begonia** x **tuberhybrida**
A fine example of the picotee begonia, which is noted for its delicate edging along the petals in a contrasting colour. An ideal bedding plant.

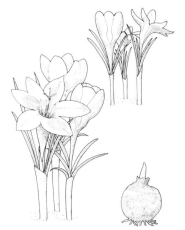

Colchicum speciosum
- Sun or partial shade
- Well-drained soil
- Plant 10-15cm/4-6in deep

This plant flowers in autumn; the flowers are white, rose, purple, violet or crimson, some with coloured veining. Leaves show in spring and last till early summer; they are 30cm/1ft long and 10cm/4in wide, four to each bulb.

It is easily cultivated in ordinary well-drained soil, and increases well in grass. Plant in early autumn. Make sure that the leaves do not choke smaller neighbours in spring. Colchicums can be grown from seed, but take up to seven years to reach flowering. Offsets from existing corms will take only two or three years to flower. Lift corms when the leaves have died down in summer, remove the offsets and replant. Keep slugs off with slug bait; the plants are usually disease-free.

Take care
Watch for slug attack on leaves and shoots.

Crocus chrysanthus 'Blue Bird'
- Sheltered sunny position
- Well-drained soil
- Plant 7.5cm/3in deep

The spring-flowering crocus has a bloom with a mauve-blue exterior edged with white, a creamy-white inside and a deep orange centre, and it flowers profusely. The short narrow leaves of pale green have a paler stripe along the spine.

These crocuses are ideal for the border or rockery, and do well in pots in a cold greenhouse. Corms can be planted in any free-draining soil. If the soil is very light, they can be planted 15cm/6in deep, but otherwise 7.5cm/3in is recommended. If crocuses are grown in grass, delay mowing until the leaves turn yellow and die back; if you cut sooner, the corms will produce very poor blooms next season. Treat the soil with a general pesticide and fungicide.

Take care
Keep the corms from becoming waterlogged.

Left: **Colchicum speciosum**
A corm that blooms after the leaves have died back, producing flowers during the autumn. It enjoys either sun or some shade.

Crocus tomasinianus
- Sunny site sheltered against cold winds
- Ordinary well-drained soil
- Plant 7.5cm/3in deep

This winter-flowering crocus has smaller flowers than the spring crocus, up to 7.5cm/3in long. The delicate blue-lavender flowers bud in winter and open in very early spring. They naturalize well in grass and sunny borders, given a sheltered position, and do well also in groups under deciduous trees or on rockeries. The varieties available are mostly deep purples such as 'Bar's Purple' and 'Whitewell Purple', but a white variety called 'Albus' is for sale from some specialists.

Corms should be planted 7.5cm/3in deep, but if the soil is very light and summer cultivation is likely to disturb the roots, they can be planted as deep as 15cm/6in. Do not remove flowers as they die, and leave foliage until it can be pulled off. Increase stock by growing the cormlets, which should flower in two years. Treat soil with a pesticide and fungicide.

Take care
Leave flowers and leaves on the plant until leaves turn yellow.

Below: **Crocus tomasinianus**
One of the first crocuses to flower, it produces blooms in late winter. The plant needs some protection to give it a good start but will then thrive in most areas of the garden.

Above: **Crocus chrysanthus 'Blue Bird'**
This crocus shows a blue bud that opens out to reveal the creamy-white inside with a deep orange centre. Thrives in full sun.

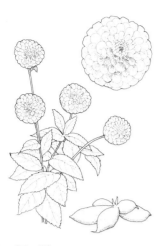

Dahlia (Ball)

- Open sunny place
- Rich well-drained soil
- Plant 10cm/4in deep

This group is noted for the ball-shaped blooms. They are fully double; the petals appear to be tubular and open out at the blunt end, and they are arranged in a spiral. The group is split into two sections: the standard ball has blooms over 10cm/4in in diameter; and the miniature ball has blooms under 10cm/4in. Both grow to 1.2m/4ft tall, and spread 75cm/30in. The colours include white, yellow, orange, red, mauve and purple.

Plant tubers in a well-drained soil which is rich in organic material, in an area that is open to the sun but sheltered from the wind; mature plants should be staked to prevent wind damage. Sprouted tubers should not be planted in the open until danger of frost has passed. Unsprouted tubers can be planted out in spring. Spray plants with a pesticide and fungicide. Wilting plants with yellow leaves must be destroyed at once.

Take care
Stake plants to keep wind damage to a minimum.

Above: **Dahlia 'Kay Helen' (Ball)**
A very neat and compact bloom that will look equally splendid in either the garden border or as a cut flower indoors.

Dahlia (Cactus)

- Open sunny site
- Rich well-drained soil
- Plant 10cm/4in deep

This group of dahlias can be divided into five sections: miniature, small, medium, large and giant. The flowers are exotic, with the petals rolled back or quilled for over half their length; the largest flowers reach up to 25cm/10in in diameter, but the smallest are only 10cm/4in. The colour range includes white, yellow, orange, red and purple, with a number of delicate shades of pink and lilac. The larger plants grow to 1.5m/5ft tall and can expand to almost 1.2m/4ft across; the smaller ones are 90cm/3ft tall and 75cm/30in across.

Tubers should preferably be planted in open sun, but will tolerate some shade. Plant them outdoors in mid-spring or start them off in a greenhouse and plant out in the late spring. Spray with a pesticide and fungicide; wilting plants with yellow leaves should be destroyed immediately as they can cause problems in spreading disease around the garden.

Take care
Winter storage of tubers must be frost-free.

Dahlia (Collarette)

- Sunny sheltered place
- Rich and moist but well-drained soil
- Plant 10cm/4in deep

This half-hardy plant will grow to 1.2m/4ft tall, with a spread of 75cm/30in. The leaves are bright green and make a good foil for the blooms, which are up to 10cm/4in across in white, yellow, orange, red or pink. The flowers have an outer ring of flat petals with an inner collar of smaller petals around the central disc of stamens. Blooms appear from late summer to the frosts in autumn, when the tuber should be lifted and stored. The following spring they can be started off in the greenhouse, and the sprouting plant put out in late spring; or the unsprouted tuber can be put out in mid-spring. The soil should be rich in organic material, compost, bonemeal or manure. Plant in full sun; shelter plants from wind or support the dahlia with a stake. Spray with a general pesticide and fungicide. Destroy plants immediately if the leaves begin wilt and turn yellow as disease can spread.

Take care
Protect dahlias against frost.

Above: **Dahlia 'Geerling's Elite' (Collarette)**
Brilliantly coloured blooms to grace any border, each with a small collar of petals around the centre. These are very free-flowering plants.

Left: **Dahlia 'Match' (Cactus)**
This is a lovely example of a multicoloured bloom, with its spiky double flowers and the petals rolled or quilled.

Dahlia (Decorative)

● Open sunny position
● Rich well-drained soil
● Plant 10cm/4in deep

This group of dahlias is distinguished by the truly double blooms of flat petals, often twisted and normally with blunt points. The group divides into five sections: giant, large, medium, small and miniature. The giants grow to 1.5m/5ft, with blooms up to 25cm/10in across; the miniatures have a height of 90cm/3ft with flowers 10cm/4in in diameter. The colours include white, yellow, orange, red, pink, purple and lavender, with some multicolours.

They all flower from late summer until the autumn frosts. Then the plants should be lifted and the tubers stored in a frost-free place until spring. Support plants with stakes, particularly the taller varieties, which are more prone to wind damage. Remove all but one bud from each stem to encourage larger blooms. Remove dead flowers to ensure further flowering. Treat the plants with a pesticide and fungicide.

Take care
Inspect tubers in winter, and destroy diseased or damaged ones.

Eranthis hyemalis

(Winter aconite)
● Sun or partial shade
● Well-drained heavy soil
● Plant 2.5cm/1in deep

This European tuberous-rooted plant grows to a height of 10cm/4in with a spread of 7.5cm/3in. The leaves are pale green and deeply cut, and the bright yellow flowers appear in late winter; in mild winters it may start blooming in midwinter. The flowers are about 2.5cm/1in across and look like buttercups but with a collar of pale green leaves just below the flower.

Plant tubers in a well-drained soil that is moist throughout the year – a heavy loam is ideal. Grow them in either sun or light shade. To propagate, lift the plant when the leaves die down, break or cut the tubers into sections, and replant these immediately, at least 7.5cm/3in apart. Seed can be sown in spring and kept in a cold frame; transplant in two years, and flowering will start after another year. Watch for bird attack. If sooty eruptions occur on the plant, destroy it to stop the spread of smut disease.

Take care
Keep soil moist in spring.

Erythronium dens-canis

(Dog's tooth violet)
● Semi-shade
● Moist well-drained soil
● Plant 7.5cm/3in deep

This cormous plant grows only 15cm/6in tall. The spotted leaves vary from plant to plant, and some are particularly attractive. The 5cm/2in flower appears in spring and the petals are folded back like a cyclamen; they are available in white, pink, red and violet, each flower having a pair of leaves up to 10cm/4in long.

Corms should be planted in autumn, preferably in groups of at least a dozen for show, in a moist but well-drained soil; choose a partially shaded site. Here they can be left for many years undisturbed. Increasing stock by growing them from seed can take over five years to reach flowering size. It is quicker to remove offsets in late summer, when the leaves have died down, and to grow them separately in a nursery bed for a year or so; they should take two years to start flowering, and then they can be planted out in autumn. Generally pest- and disease-free.

Take care
Keep these plants moist.

Left: Dahlia 'Yma Sumac' (Decorative)
These dahlias are recognized by the characteristic double blooms with the petals often twisted. A wide choice of sizes is available.

Above: **Eranthis hyemalis**
A ground-hugging plant with brilliant yellow flowers that look like buttercups. It thrives in a heavy soil that is moist throughout the year.

Below: **Erythronium dens-canis**
A low-growing plant that has beautifully marked leaves and delicate blooms that appear in spring and continue into summer. Needs some shade.

Erythronium tuolumnense

● Shady situation
● Moist but not waterlogged soil
● Plant 10cm/4in deep

This plant grows to 30cm/1ft, with a spread of 15cm/6in. It has bright green leaves that are broad and pointed. The spring flowers have six pointed yellow petals and are like small lilies.

The corms should be planted 10cm/4in deep, in a moist but not boggy soil that has plenty of leaf-mould to keep it well drained, and with some shade. They should be planted in late summer and can be left undisturbed until they become overcrowded; then lift, divide and replant when the leaves die down in summer. Seed takes over five years to reach flowering; it is quicker to increase stock from offsets, which reach flowering in three years. Make sure the soil does not dry out when plants are young, as they need constantly moist soil to thrive. A good layer of well-rotted manure or compost spread over the plants in autumn keeps the organic level high.

Take care
Keep the soil moist (but not wet) until plants are established.

Right: **Freesia 'Red Star'**
Although normally grown under glass, some varieties are available for outdoor use. All have highly coloured and scented flowers and sword-like leaves. Plant corms in spring.

Left: **Erythronium tuolumnense**
This plant loves a moist soil and shade, where it will flower in spring with yellow lily-like blooms. It likes to be left alone and undisturbed; a woodland site is ideal.

Above: **Galanthus nivalis**
Normally flowering in midwinter, the low-growing snowdrop is often regarded as the herald of spring. It will grow best in light shade and a good soil that is moist and free-draining. Handle bulbs with care.

Freesia x hybrida
(F. x kewensis)
- **Sheltered sunny position**
- **Light sandy soil**
- **Plant 5cm/2in deep**

These plants grow to 45cm/18in tall, with a spread of 15cm/6in. The leaves are narrow and sword-like, and the flower stems have spikes of scented trumpet-shaped 5cm/2in blooms in summer. Although most are suitable for the greenhouse only, some are available for growing out of doors, being planted in spring to flower in the summer of the first season only. A wide variety of colours is available, from white through yellow to pink, red, magenta and violet.

Freesias need a light sandy soil and a position that is sunny and sheltered from cold winds. Plant the corms in spring unless you have a frost-free area, where they can be planted in late summer to flower the following spring. After flowering the corms can be lifted and treated as greenhouse bulbs where they can provide flowers in early spring, but they need a minimum temperature of 5°C/41°F. Offsets removed in late summer flower the following year.

Take care
Protect from frost.

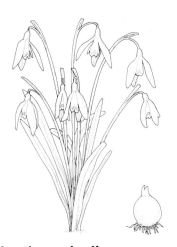

Galanthus nivalis
(Snowdrop)
- **Partial shade**
- **Rich well-drained soil**
- **Plant 10-15cm/4-6cm deep**

Snowdrop leaves are flat, sword-shaped and often blue-green in colour. The flowers are either single or double, in white with green markings on the inner petals, and can be as long as 2.5cm/1in. Snowdrops' time of flowering depends on the severity or mildness of the winter weather but normally starts around midwinter. One variety flowers in late autumn, before the leaves appear. They can grow up to 20cm/8in tall in rich soil and in partial shade.

The bulbs should be planted 10cm/4in deep in heavy soil, or 15cm/6in deep in light soil, in autumn; the soil should be moist but well drained. Move bulbs after they have finished flowering, while the soil is moist. Seed may take five years to bloom, so it is better to split clusters of bulbs and spread them out. Take care when lifting not to damage the roots or let them dry out. Use a soil insecticide and fungicide.

Take care
Leave bulbs undisturbed for several years for improved flowering.

Gladiolus (Large-flowered)
- Full sun
- Ordinary garden soil with added humus
- Plant 10-15cm/4-6in deep

The large-flowered gladiolus hybrids are half-hardy plants that need some protection against frost. The plants often reach 1.2m/4ft high. The flower spike is about 50cm/20in long, and individual blooms are 17.5cm/7in across. They flower in summer, in vivid shades of white, yellow, orange, red, purple, rust, pink and mauve, either with markings or plain.

These hybrids are easily grown from corms planted 10-15cm/4-6in deep; in lighter soils plant at the greater depth. Put some sharp sand under the corms to aid drainage, and place in full sun. An ordinary garden soil with some manure added is ideal. As they mature, the plants may become top-heavy, so staking is useful. When the plant dies back after flowering, lift it and store the new corm in a frost-free place for the following year. Treat with pesticide and fungicide to keep plants healthy.

Take care
Protect against frost and excessive wetness.

Above: **Gladiolus 'Aristocrat'**
One of the large-flowered varieties available in brilliant colours. By staggering the planting you can have blooms throughout the summer.

Above: **Gladiolus 'Nanus Minetto'**
*A miniature hybrid gladiolus with delicate form
and finely marked blooms. These look well in
flower arrangements and also in the garden
border, ideally near the front.*

Hymenocallis x festalis
(Spider lily)
- **Full sun, sheltered from frost**
- **Rich well-drained soil**
- **Plant with top just level with surface**

This plant is susceptible to frost; unless your
garden has a near frost-free climate, treat it as a
pot plant. The white scented flowers, 10cm/4in
across, have a centre not unlike a daffodil
trumpet, but the outer petals are long and
slender. The strap-like leaves are 30cm/1ft long.
The plant grows to 45cm/18in tall, and blooms in
spring if grown as a pot plant; out of doors it
flowers in summer.

When growing this as a pot plant use a
medium or large pot with a general potting
mixture. For early blooms keep it at 16°C/60°F,
but for later flowers keep the greenhouse just
frost-free. In spring give a mild liquid feed every
two weeks. Keep it in shade, and water well in
hot weather; repot every two or three years. For
outdoors grow it in a pot and plant out in late
spring in a well-drained soil in full sun. Generally
this plant is trouble-free.

Take care
Protect from frost.

Gladiolus (Miniature hybrids)
- **Sunny position**
- **Good well-drained garden soil**
- **Plant 10-15cm/4-6in deep**

These plants grow to 45-90cm/18-36in tall, and
the flower spikes are about 35cm/14in long, with
each flower about 5cm/2in across. They bloom
after midsummer, and flowers are often frilled or
fluted. The colours are bright, and varied with
blotches, spots and stripes.

These corms are best grown in a sunny part of
the garden in a good well-drained soil; they
should be planted 10-15cm/4-6in deep,
depending on the soil – plant deeper in light soil
to give better anchorage. In heavy soil, add
plenty of sharp sand under and around the corm
to aid drainage, keep the young plant weeded,
and water well once the flower spike starts to
open. Lift the plant in autumn, remove the young
corm and store it in a frost-free place for the
following year. Keep the plant free from disease
with a fungicide; if the plant wilts and turns
yellow, destroy it to stop the virus disease
spreading to others.

Take care
Do not grow in waterlogged soil.

Below: **Hymenocallis x festalis**
*A scented summer-flowering plant that has a
narcissus-like trumpet and long slender petals. A
trouble-free plant which will grow in full sun.*

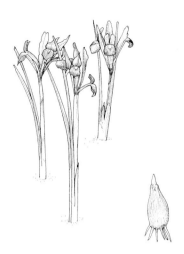

Iris (Reticulata / I. reticulata var.)
(Bulbous irises)
- Light shade or sun
- Light well-drained limy soil
- Plant 5-7.5cm/2-3in deep

These hardy Asian bulbous plants have a net of fibres around the outside of the bulb and grass-like tubular leaves that are dark green with a paler tip. They are early flowering; some start at midwinter and others follow successively through to spring. The flowers are often 7.5cm/3in wide, in lemon-yellow and blue. These plants are small, and ideal for the rock garden; they rarely grow more than 15cm/6in tall.

Plant them in a light well-drained chalky soil; if the ground is heavy, the bulb may not shoot after the first year. Give each bulb a covering of 5-7.5cm/2-3in of soil. They do best when planted in autumn. After flowering give a liquid feed every four weeks until the bulb dies back. If grown for indoor decoration, plant them in pots, keep in the cool until the flower buds show, then bring into the warm. Use a fungicide and pesticide to keep the plants healthy.

Take care
Do not plant in heavy moist soil.

Lilium Asiatic cultivars
- Full sun or semi-shade
- Well-drained garden soil
- Plant 10-15cm/4-6in deep

These are early-flowering lilies with blooms growing either singly or in groups springing from the same point on the stem. These cultivars grow up to 1.5m/5ft tall, with some flowers reaching 15cm/6in across. Some forms have hanging flowers with petals curled back to form a 'Turk's cap'. Blooms appear at midsummer with a variety of colours, shapes and markings.

The bulbs should be planted 10-15cm/4-6in deep in well-drained garden soil, in full sun or semi-shade, during the winter months. During the growing season they should be kept moist with plenty of water and mulching with peat, compost or leaf-mould.

Every few years the plants can be lifted in the winter months, divided and replanted with more space around them. Seed will take up to three years to reach flowering. The plants should be treated with a general pesticide and fungicide.

Take care
It is important to keep plants moist during the growing period.

Left: **Iris reticulata 'Jeanine'**
A bulbous iris that is very popular for the rock garden and border. It blooms in late winter and early spring and prefers a light chalky soil. Also suitable for growing indoors.

Narcissus cyclamineus
● Sun or partial shade
● Moist well-drained soil
● Plant 5cm/2in deep

Like all members of the narcissus and daffodil family, this species has the typical cup and petals, but the petals are turned back. The plant comes from Spain and Portugal, is small, only 20cm/8in tall, and the trumpets are 5cm/2in long. This dwarf habit makes it ideal for the rock garden, where its fine delicate form and dark green grass-like leaves keep it in scale with other low-growing plants. The yellow flowers bloom in early spring, and do equally well in the open or in partial shade providing the soil is moist.

Plant the bulbs 5cm/2in deep and 5cm/2in apart. They will seed themselves, or in late summer they can be lifted, divided and replanted to allow more space. Treat the plants with a pesticide and fungicide to keep troubles to a minimum, but if damage is bad it is better to destroy the plant.

Take care
Keep soil moist in dry periods.

Above: **Lilium 'Enchantment'**
A vigorous Asiatic lily with up to 16 outstanding cup-shaped flowers to a stem. Enjoys a sunny position and a well-drained soil.

Below: **Narcissus cyclamineus**
An early spring-flowering dwarf that makes an ideal rockery plant, where its unusual petals and grass-like leaves can be appreciated.

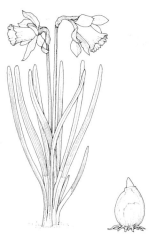

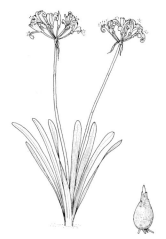

Narcissus pseudonarcissus
(Lent lily, Wild daffodil)
- Sun or light shade
- Moist soil
- Plant 5cm/2in deep

This plant has strap-like leaves, and grows to a height of 30cm/1ft. The flowers have bright lemon trumpets with very pale yellow petals 5cm/2in across, and appear in spring. They thrive in a good moist soil, among low grass or in open woodland. They are good for naturalizing where a small daffodil will be in scale.

This species is easy to grow in a moist soil, and will be happy in either sun or light shade, where it should be planted at a depth of 5cm/2in. If the soil and the situation are to its liking, it will thrive and spread vigorously, forming clumps. After a few years it is advisable to lift the bulbs after the leaves have died back, divide them and replant with 7.5cm/3in between bulbs. A more natural look is obtained by casting the bulbs over the area and planting them where they have fallen. Use a pesticide and fungicide to keep plants healthy.

Take care
Be sure to keep the plants moist, especially in hot weather.

Nerine bowdenii
(Guernsey lily)
- Sunny position
- Ordinary well-drained soil
- Plant just under the surface

Nerine bowdenii, which comes from South Africa, is sufficiently hardy to withstand most winters in the temperate zone. It will grow to a height of 60cm/2ft. The blooms open in autumn, with up to eight flowers in each cluster; the clusters are 15cm/6in across, usually rose or deep pink, but there is also a white form. The mid-green leaves are narrow and strap-like.

The bulbs should be planted in either late summer or early spring, and in an ordinary well-drained soil and in a sunny position. The bulbs are placed just under the surface or, if the soil is light, they can be set deeper – as much as 10cm/4in. Where there are bulbs near the surface they should be covered with a thick layer of bracken, leaf-mould or compost to protect them against frost. They can be lifted in spring, divided and replanted to encourage larger blooms. Watch for mealy bugs and treat them with pesticide.

Take care
Keep moist when growing.

Below: **Nerine bowdenii**
This fine showy plant bears lovely deep pink flowers in autumn. It enjoys a warm sunny border backed with a wall for protection against cold winds and frosts.

Left: **Narcissus pseudonarcissus**
A small narcissus that naturalizes well in light woodland or in grass, where its blooms can be enjoyed in spring. Plant in moist soil.

Right: **Ornithogalum umbellatum**
Hardy and requiring little attention, this plant is ideal for edgings around beds and borders and also for mass effects. Needs a well-drained soil and can thrive in partial shade.

Ornithogalum umbellatum
(Dove's dung, Nap-at-noon, Star of Bethlehem, Summer snowflake)
● **Partial shade**
● **Ordinary well-drained soil**
● **Plant 7.5cm/3in deep**

This plant grows to a height of 30cm/2ft, with a spread of up to 20cm/8in. In spring, the flower stem carries a profusion of white star-like blooms with green stripes on the outside. The plant is hardy, and is ideal for edgings and for mass effects, even naturalizing in short grass or in the shrubbery.

Plant the bulbs in autumn, in ordinary well-drained soil with 7.5cm/3in of soil over them in an area where there is some shade; if possible, dig in a good quantity of peat, compost or leaf-mould beforehand. Once planted they need no attention and will continue to produce masses of blossom. To increase stock, lift the clumps of bulbs in late summer after the leaves have died down, divide them, and replant with more space. Seeds can be sown, but take up to four years to reach flowering size. Most ornithogalums are pest-free, but watch for fungus attack on leaves.

Take care
Keep plants moist in droughts.

Above: **Rhodohypoxis baurii 'Margaret Rose'**
Flowering from spring though to the autumn, these South African plants require a well-drained soil and a sunny position.

Below: **Scilla tubergeniana**
A pale scilla that blooms as soon as it emerges from the soil in the late winter. This low-growing plant is ideal for rock gardens.

Rhodohypoxis baurii
- Full sun
- Well-drained moist soil
- Plant just below the surface

These South African plants grow to only 7.5cm/3in high, with a spread of 15cm/6in, and they have hairy pale sword-like leaves. The flowers have six petals, the three inner ones standing a fraction higher than the three outer ones; blooms vary from white to deep red, 3cm/1.25in in diameter, and appear from spring through to autumn.

Plant the corm-like rhizomes in autumn in a well-drained but moisture-retentive lime-free soil, with a good sunny position. In wet winters, put a cloche over the plants to keep them dry, and it will also give some protection against frost. Lift the plant in autumn to remove the offsets; replant these and they should flower the following year. Where excessive cold and damp occurs, treat them as pot plants. Grow them in 15cm/6in pots of well-drained lime-free mixture, watering frequently until the autumn; then repot and allow them to almost dry out. Give water as the plant begins shooting.

Take care
Avoid excessive wetness in winter.

Scilla tubergeniana
- Sun or semi-shade
- Moist well-drained soil
- Plant 5cm/2in deep

This scilla comes from the mountainous meadows and rocks of north-west Iran and grows to a height of 10cm/4in, with a similar spread. The flowers it produces are pale blue or white in colour, and open up as soon as they emerge from the soil.

The bulbs should be planted as soon as they are purchased, in late summer or early autumn, in a sunny or half-shaded area of the garden where the soil is moist but well-drained. Cover the bulbs with 5cm/2in of soil. For a casual effect the bulbs can be cast gently over the area and planted where they fall.

To increase the moisture-holding properties of the soil dig in a good supply of leaf-mould, peat or compost before planting. Once planted the bulbs can be left untouched, but to increase stock offsets can be taken from mature plants after the leaves have died down, and placed in a nursery bed to grow. Seed may take up to five years to reach flowering size.

Take care
Keep moist in dry weather.

Left: **Sprekelia formosissima**
A most unusual flower is produced by this half-hardy plant from Mexico. It enjoys full sun or light shade and a rich soil. It can be used for outdoor show, but give it some protection against cold winds and frost.

Sprekelia formosissima
(Amaryllis formosissima)
- **Full light or light shade**
- **Rich potting mixture**
- **Plant with neck just above soil**

This Mexican half-hardy plant is grown as a pot plant for its funnel-shaped deep-red flowers. It grows 45cm/18in tall with sparse strap-like leaves that appear after flowering has finished. The flower stems appear in spring, each stem bearing only one flower, 10cm/4in wide.

Plant bulbs singly in 10cm/4in pots of rich potting mixture such as John Innes No. 3 in late summer, with the neck of the bulb just above the surface. Keep the temperature over 8°C/45°F. Do not water until spring, then water with a liquid feed every two weeks from flowering until the leaves die back in summer. Repot in early autumn every few years, and at this time remove offsets and plant them in separate pots; they take up to four years to reach flowering.

Look out for white tufts of waxy wool at the base of the leaves, caused by the mealy bug: use a systemic pesticide to clear the attack.

Take care
Keep dry in autumn.

Sternbergia lutea
*(Lily of the field, Winter daffodil,
Yellow star flower)*
● **Full sun**
● **Well-drained soil**
● **Plant 10-15cm/4-6in deep**

This plant from the eastern Mediterranean and
Iran looks like a crocus but flowers in autumn,
with bright blooms up to 5cm/2in long on a true
stem. The strap-like leaves appear with the
flower but remain small and immature until the
following spring. The plant will reach a height of
15cm/6in, with a similar spread.

Plant the bulbs in late summer, 10-15cm/4-6in
deep in a well-drained soil, in a sunny part of the
garden. Leave undisturbed until they become
overcrowded, when they can be lifted in late
summer, divided and replanted immediately to
prevent drying out. The offsets can be removed
and grown separately, and will mature and come
into flower in one year. This plant can be grown
with, or as an alternative to, autumn-flowering
crocuses and will provide a show of brilliant
yellow. If slugs attack the young growth, use a
slug bait. Normally this plant is disease-free.

Take care
Leave undisturbed if possible.

Above: **Sternbergia lutea**
*An autumn-flowering plant that looks like a
crocus and gives a show of brilliant yellow
flowers. An ideal subject for the rock garden.*

Below: **Tigridia pavonia 'Rubra'**
*A succession of vivid and unusual blooms
adorns this plant in summer. The strange
markings justify its common name of tiger flower.*

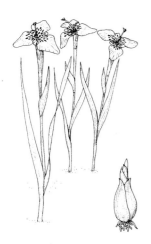

Tigridia pavonia
(Peacock tiger flower, Tiger flower)
- Sunny location
- Rich well-drained soil
- Plant 7.5-10cm/3-4in deep

These spectacular half-hardy plants from Mexico and Peru can reach 60cm/2ft tall, with long sword-shaped pleated leaves of mid-green. The flowers last only a day, but each stem produces a succession of up to eight blooms in summer. These are up to 10cm/4in wide, and have three large petals with three small petals in between, surrounding a cup-shaped base; the larger petals are plain but the smaller ones are spotted in white, yellow or red, which gives them the common name of tiger flower.

Plant the corms in spring, 7.5-10cm/3-4in deep in a rich well-drained soil, in a position where there is plenty of sun. Lift them in autumn and keep dry and frost-free until replanting time next spring. At this time cormlets can be removed and grown separately, to reach flowering size in a couple of years. During winter guard against mice eating the stored corms.

Take care
Keep moist in dry weather.

Tulip Division 1: Single Early
- Full sun
- Slightly alkaline soil
- Plant 15cm/6in deep at most

Tulips were introduced into Europe from Turkey over 300 years ago and an industry for developing bulbs and hybrids has centred in the Netherlands since that time.

The single early is self-descriptive: single blooms in spring when grown out of doors, or in winter if forced under glass. The flowers grow to 12.5cm/5in wide, and sometimes open flat in direct sunshine. A wide range of colours is available, in white, yellow, pink, red, orange, purple and mixtures. The plants, 15-38cm/6-15in tall, are ideal for bedding or border planting.

Plant in the late autumn in a slightly alkaline soil, in full sunlight, 15cm/6in deep. When the petals fall, cut off the head to allow the leaves and stem to feed the bulb for the following season. Offsets can be removed during the late autumn and grown on. Use a pesticide and fungicide.

Take care
Dead-head the plants to build up the bulbs for next year.

A NOTE ON TULIPS

In total there are 15 divisions of Tulip but lack of space in this book has precluded the inclusion of complete details on each. For reference purposes a listing of each division is given below:

Division 1: Single Early
Division 2: Double Early
Division 3: Mendel
Division 4: Triumph
Division 5: Darwin Hybrids
Division 6: Darwin
Division 7: Lily-flowered
Division 8: Cottage
Division 9: Rembrandt
Division 10: Parrot
Division 11: Double Late
Division 12: Kaufmanniana varieties
Division 13: Fosteriana varieties
Division 14: Greigii varieties
Division 15: Species

Above: **Tulip 'Hadley' (Division 1)**
The large-flowered, single early bloom comes in the spring and makes a good subject for formal bedding and border layouts.

Tulip Division 2: Double Early
● Full sun
● Alkaline soil
● Plant 15cm/6in deep at most

This group of tulips has early-blooming flowers in spring, and if forced under glass can be in flower in late winter. The form is double, with blooms often reaching 10cm/4in across. The plants grow to 30-38cm/12-15in, and leaves are often grey-green. A good example is 'Orange Nassau', a large blood-red tulip ideal for bedding out or forcing. The colours most readily available are white, yellow, pink, orange, red, violet and purple, with many multicolours.

Plant out bulbs in late autumn in a slightly alkaline soil, 15cm/6in deep. Tulips thrive in direct sunlight. When the petals fall, dead-head the plant but leave the stem and leaves to feed the bulb for the coming season. When the leaves turn yellow the plant can be lifted and stored for replanting in late autumn. Offsets can be taken at lifting time and grown on. Treat the plant with pesticide and fungicide.

Take care
Keep moist while growing.

Tulip Division 3: Mendel
● Full sun
● Ordinary soil that is not acid
● Plant 15cm/6in deep at most

These tulips flower later than Divisions 1 and 2 and the blooms are more rounded, some 12.5cm/5in across, and borne on slender stems. They flower in mid-spring, and colours include white, yellow, red and deep red. Representative of this division is 'Athleet', a lovely white tulip. Plants grow to a height of 50cm/20in, and the mid-green or blue-green leaves are shaped like a broad spear-head.

They enjoy an alkaline soil in full sun. Plant bulbs in late autumn at a depth of 15cm/6in, and water in well if the soil is dry. Keep moist during the growing period. When the petals fall, cut off the flowerhead to stop goodness concentrating on seed production to the detriment of the bulb. Bulbs can be lifted when the leaves turn yellow; remove offsets and grow on separately. The parent bulb can be dried and stored for replanting in late autumn. Treat the plants with a pesticide and fungicide.

Take care
Keep moist while growing.

Tulip Division 4: Triumph
● Sunny position
● Slightly alkaline soil
● Plant 15cm/6in deep at most

These tulips grow to 50cm/20in, and flower in mid-season, after the early singles and doubles but at the same time as the Mendel tulips in mid-spring. The blooms have an angular look and are carried on sturdy stems. The colours include white, yellow, orange, gold, pink, red and lilac. An example of this group is 'Garden Party', a white flower edged with pink.

These tulips thrive in a slightly alkaline soil in full sun. Bulbs should be planted at a depth of 15cm/6in in late autumn; in light soils increase the depth to provide anchorage. Water in the bulbs and keep them moist during the growing period. After flowering cut the heads off to keep the nutrients feeding the bulb. When leaves turn yellow the plant can be lifted; remove offsets and grow on separately. Store the parent bulb in a dry place to ripen, before replanting during the late autumn. Use both a pesticide and a fungicide to prevent attacks.

Take care
Keep dead-heading plants.

Left: **Tulip 'Trance' (Division 3)**
A Mendel tulip which blooms in mid-spring. It prefers a sunny site where there is some lime in the soil. It grows to a height of 50cm/20in.

Right: **Tulip 'Montgomery' (Division 3)**
These distinctive Mendel tulips, with striking margins, would grace any garden border. Keep them moist during the growing period.

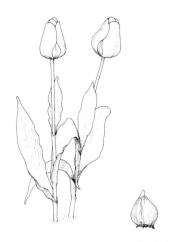
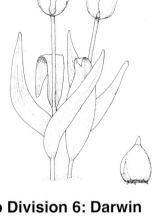

Tulip Division 5: Darwin Hybrids

- Full sun
- Slightly alkaline soil
- Plant 15cm/6in deep at most

The tulips in this group are among the most brilliant and large-flowered. The leaves are grey-green and the plant grows over 60cm/2ft tall. Blooms reach 17.5cm/7in wide when they open in mid-spring. The colours include yellow, orange, red and purple, with some spectacular multicoloured flowers. 'Golden Oxford' (a pure yellow), 'Big Chief' (one of the larger tulips grown, 65cm/26in tall, with rose-coloured flowers) and 'Beauty of Apeldoorn' (a creamy-yellow flushed with orange, with black base and anthers) are tulips that fall into this section.

These plants enjoy a slightly alkaline soil in full sun, and bulbs should be planted 15cm/6in deep in late autumn. If the soil is dry, water well in and keep moist during the growing period. When the flowers have finished, cut off the heads to allow the stem and leaves to feed the bulb. Lift when the leaves turn yellow, remove offsets and plant separately.

Take care
In acid soils add lime or chalk.

Tulip Division 6: Darwin

- Full sun
- Good soil that is not acid
- Plant 15cm/6in deep at most

Within this group are the most popular bedding tulips, growing 75cm/30in tall, with mid-green to blue-green leaves. The flowers are rounded and often reach 12.5cm/5in across, blooming in late spring after the hybrids. Colours include white, yellow, orange, pink, red and purple, with a number of dramatic multicoloured varieties. Among many named tulips available are: 'Bleu Aimable' (lilac flushed with purple, and a blue base); 'Snowpeak' (pure white); and 'La Tulipe Noire' (deep purple-black).

These tulips thrive in good garden soil that is not acid; acid soil needs added lime or chalk to make it more alkaline. Choose a sunny position, with 15cm/6in of soil over the bulbs, which should be planted in late autumn. Keep them moist during the growing period. When the flowers fade, cut off the heads. When the leaves die lift the plant; remove offsets and replant them, storing the parent bulb until late autumn.

Take care
Keep moist while growing.

Right: **Tulip 'Orajezon' (Division 6)**
These popular bedding Darwin tulips bloom in late spring. They perform best in full sun and require a soil which is not acid.

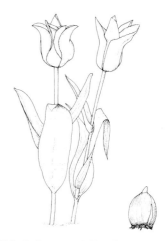

Tulip Division 7: Lily-flowered

● **Full sun**
● **Slightly alkaline soil**
● **Plant 15cm/6in deep at most**

These tulips are noted for their flower shape, being slightly waisted with pointed petals that curl outwards. Blooms open in mid-spring and often reach 20cm/8in wide. The leaves are green, some with a grey cast; the plants reach 60cm/2ft tall, and look very effective when massed in the border.

Colours include white, yellow, orange, red and multicoloured variations. Notable examples are 'Golden Duchess' (deep primrose yellow), 'Mariette' (deep rose, with a glorious texture to the petals), 'Picotee' (white, with a deep rose edging that increases in area as the plant ages) and 'White Triumphator' (a long white bloom).

These tulips enjoy full sun and a slightly alkaline soil. Plant 15cm/6in deep in a sunny place in late autumn, and keep it moist while growing. Once the flower petals fall, cut off the heads. When leaves turn yellow, lift the plant, remove the offsets and grow them separately until mature. Use a pesticide and fungicide.

Take care
Add lime to an acid soil.

Left: **Tulip 'Aladdin' (Division 7)**
This is a lily-flowered tulip with typical waisted bloom and pointed petals. Flowering from mid-spring, they need a slightly alkaline soil.

Part Four: Alpines

Introduction

A rock garden – and the plants which go with it – can add a focus of interest to every garden, no matter how large or small. This section deals with those plants and flowers most likely to give a range of colour through the year.

To choose a small number of alpines, out of a total of several thousand that could be grown, might appear at first to be a daunting task. It is certainly invidious to have to exclude some of the most attractive genera, but as the main criterion was the availability of the subjects in commerce, the exclusion of some of the rarer and more challenging plants was rendered somewhat easier, and reduced the list to more manageable proportions. Also excluded are any alpines that are tender, although there may be one or two borderline plants that in harsher climes could tend to curl up their toes at extreme temperatures.

However, the plants given here are, in general, basically hardy. Among the plants described there are several genera of which only a representative selection can be included. The campanulas, saxifrages and gentians come to mind, along with *Dianthus*, *Phlox* and *Primula*; these would all repay wider study for the variation that is to be found within their ranks, in terms of colour, texture and varying forms.

Dwarf shrubs have been scantily dealt with in the text. There are many that help to provide a strong background for the rock garden, such as *Berberis x stenophylla* 'Corallina Compacta', which is a perfect essay in miniaturization of the larger forms. The dwarf willows bring interest in the late winter with their catkins, and *Salix x boydii* provides a variation with its grey woolly leaves.

To dismiss a potential misunderstanding, the terms *alpine* and *rock plant* are synonymous. Consideration should be given at this point to the actual rock garden itself – the term *rock garden* being infinitely preferable to *rockery*.

The rock garden

The basic material, rock, is very expensive these days, and economical use must be made of the material available. It is also harmful to the natural habitat to use natural stone. Substitutes are available, such as concrete, and these should be considered. It is not necessary to have a steep slope on which the rock garden can be built. It is possible to create one on a perfectly flat site, by excavating paths and piling up the excavated soil to make the rock garden. My own practice is to create a gentle slope and then arrange the rock on the outcrop principle. To go back to basics for a moment: all rock starts off as a solid lump; nature then fractures it horizontally and vertically. In practice this means that one does not interlock rock as in a brick wall; rather, the lines should follow each other.

The outcrop principle creates individual beds, which can then take different soil mixtures to accommodate the varying needs of certain plants.

No rock garden should be completed in a hurry, for trouble is bound to follow. It is essential to remove all perennial weeds from the site, resorting to chemical means if they are persistent; this advice cannot be emphasized too much, even if it does sound boring. Neither should there be any hurry to plant, as the ground needs time to settle down. Ideally, the rock garden should be constructed in autumn, and left to settle over the winter. Planting can then take place during the following spring.

What sort of rock should be chosen? For practical, economic and aesthetic reasons it should be the rock that is quarried nearest to the site of your garden. If you are in a sandstone area do not choose limestone or vice versa, as it will look wrong. There is a lightweight substance called *tufa*, which is formed in some limestone areas. This is a porous material and much beloved by some plants, because they can get their fine roots into it.

Alpines do not have to be grown on a rock garden. An alternative is the raised bed, built of rock to whatever height is required. It is a most practical idea for elderly or wheelchair gardeners, as the plants are brought up to a comfortable working level. Trailing plants can cascade over the sides and those requiring good drainage can be planted on top. Such beds as these can also be constructed with old railway sleepers or concrete blocks, though the latter do not have quite the natural look about them.

The peat bed

The peat bed is constantly referred to and this is very much a man-made concept. The ideal situation is near water, in order to give a buoyant atmosphere. Here the rule about building a brick wall can apply, as interlocking gives strength to the peat blocks if they have to be raised at all. Some experts suggest that it is possible to create a peat garden for acid-loving plants above an alkaline soil. My view is that you should not be trying to defeat nature all the time: if you live in an alkaline or chalky area, then accept the fact and grow what does well in your area, rather than settle for miserable plants struggling to live in adverse conditions.

The peat garden is for acid-loving plants and those that require cool moist conditions. Some shade, but not a total overcast, is also required, where plants can be protected from intense sun, particularly at midday in high summer. The dappled sunshine that filters through a deciduous tree is ideal. The peat garden can be separate or part of the general rock garden if the situation lends itself. Dwarf rhododendrons are very useful subjects, as there is such a vast selection of colour and form to choose from.

The terms *alkaline* and *acid* are used very frequently. These are the extremes of the pH scale, on which 7 is considered to be neutral: anything below 7 is acidic, and above is alkaline. In practice it is rare to find a pH greater than 8.5 or lower than 4.5, although some moorland soils can go down to 3.5 or lower. No ericaceous plant will tolerate any alkalinity much above a pH of 6.5, but plants that tolerate a high pH will sometimes grow in acid conditions.

Troughs and sinks

Reference is occasionally made in the text to a plant's suitability for planting in a trough or sink. The ideal is the natural stone sink originally used in old cottages. In days gone by these could be obtained cheaply, but nowadays they have become almost collectors' items. These sinks can accommodate the real miniatures and are a delight in a particularly small area or on a terrace or patio. It is not possible for everyone to obtain a natural stone trough, so a substance called *hypertufa* was invented some years ago. This is a mixture of sand: peat: cement in the ratio of 1:2:1 to give a tufa-like finish, or 2.5:1.5:1 to give a sandstone finish. A trough can be made entirely of this substance by placing a layer of the mixture in the base of a cardboard box, placing another, but smaller, box on top of this layer; this should leave a gap all around, which is then filled with more of the mixture and left. The 'give' of the cardboard boxes will provide some irregularity to the trough's appearance.

Alternatively, a glazed sink can be coated with the hypertufa, using an industrial adhesive. This can be a tricky operation, but a thin layer (5-10mm/0.2-0.4in) is spread on after coating the glazed sink with adhesive. It can be 'chipped' when almost dry to give a natural look.

Propagating frames

In the text, propagating frames are mentioned; these can be sited outside, either free-standing or against the walls of a house, shed or greenhouse. A sand frame is made up from pure sharp sand, kept moist, into which any cutting is inserted. Some plants prefer a cooler, damper medium, in which case the peat frame is recommended, with just a smattering of sand to keep it 'open'. Whatever the mixture, there is always a glass frame over it, to conserve the heat and to control the water supply. Ideally, the cuttings should be no more than 15cm/6in away from the glass; tall cuttings are inserted at the back, as most frames are sloping. Sometimes propagating frames are placed in a greenhouse, and this offers double protection to less hardy subjects, but care should be taken that these cuttings are not drawn up by the combination of glass and heat.

Pinching out is a term used after propagation takes place. This simply involves the removal of the central growing point, in order to encourage the plant to sprout lateral shoots and in general to keep it looking neat and tidy.

Growing alpines from seed

Seed sowing is a straightforward operation, with less mystique than some tend to attach to it. The main thing is to choose the right type of container, i.e. clay or plastic and the correct size for the job.

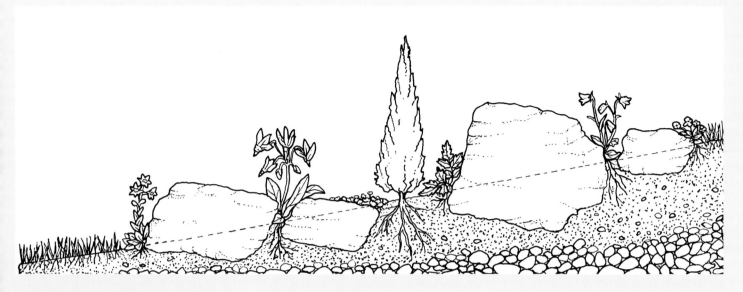

Above: The rock garden
This cross-section shows how the drainage materials and soil layers have been built up into a gentle slope and the rocks positioned as natural-looking outcrops.

Remember that plastic pots can easily be overwatered. Fill the pot to the brim with compost, tapping the pot to settle the compost; then, with another pot, press the mixture firmly so that there is a gap of about 6-7mm/0.24-0.28in from the rim. Sow the seeds thinly; this is most important, as crowded seedlings are prone to damping off. Then cover with either sharp sand or chippings, according to the fineness of the seeds sown. Stand the pot in a bowl of water, with the level of water lower than the rim of the pot, until the surface of the soil glistens with moisture; you will then know that it has percolated through.

Seeds and potting composts need a short explanation. There are two basic forms of these composts: the well-tried and well-known John Innes formula, and the peat-based Arthur Bowyers, the latter being more suitable for ericaceous and peat-loving plants. In commerce, John Innes composts are extremely variable, but certain brands are specially formulated for alpines and should be sought out. Limestone and granite chippings can be added to the compost to cater for any plant's particular requirement: most saxifrages, for instance, thrive on good drainage and enjoy limestone chippings.

Always label seed pots with a reliable pen or indelible pencil, as some alpine seeds may not germinate for a year or two. If they have not germinated in the first season, leave the pot out to be frosted the following winter, to see if that will assist germination.

In general, it is sensible to label plants on the rock garden, but a forest of white labels is not an attractive sight, so try to choose a less obtrusive type of plant marker.

The alpine house
The alpine house is every enthusiast's eventual dream. It is devised to house plants that are not so much tender, as more in need of protection from adverse overhead weather, such as winter rain. No heating is necessary, and in fact considerable extra ventilation must be supplied to prevent a stagnant atmosphere from encouraging disease. It is only in the severest weather that the alpine house is shut up completely. Here can be grown some of the most challenging and difficult plants from the world's mountains. It is also a good place to be if the weather is too bad to garden outside or some unpleasant domestic chore needs to be forgotten.

Pests and diseases
It would be repetitious to keep stating that no particular pests attack each of the plants described, so a general note is included here to mention one or two. Greenfly, and aphids in general, can be a nuisance, particularly after a mild winter; there are several effective sprays on the market to deal with them. At least greenfly can be seen with comparative ease, but the hidden pest chewing away at the underground parts of a plant is difficult to trace and to eradicate. One such is the vine weevil larva, which eats roots – particularly those of primulas; the first indication of its presence is the sudden deterioration of the plants. On investigation, the grubs will be found in the soil; aldrin or lindane dust will control this pest, which may attack other plants if in pots in a greenhouse. Root aphids sometimes attack the European primulas, such as *P. auricula*, and malathion is the control here. Otherwise, apart from the possibility of slugs, it can generally be said that alpines are comparatively pest- and disease-free.

Expanding the interest
Rock gardening is almost a disease, for if it gets hold of you there is no cure! As your enthusiasm increases, you will want to propagate plants – not only to replenish any gaps in your garden, but to exchange with others. There is nothing more pleasant for the visitor than to depart with a handful of plants. You may then wish to progress to an alpine house, where the treasures of the high mountains can be housed. When you are really hooked, there is the possibility of exhibiting at one of the specialist shows.

In this short introduction it is possible to mention only a few points, but one final remark must be made about bulbs on the rock garden. They are absolutely invaluable and can provide a colourful show, so ensure you do not overlook their tremendous potential.

All this has touched only very lightly on a vast subject. I hope you are inspired to continue and deepen your interest.

Michael Upward

A-Z Index by Latin Name

Aethionema 'Warley Ruber'
(Stone cress)
- **Full sun**
- **Any well-drained soil**
- **Evergreen sub-shrub**

The shrubby, hardy aethionemas give of their best in a hot dry situation on the rock garden. They thrive on sunny limestone in the Mediterranean region, but in cultivation will tolerate a neutral soil. They form neat plants of bushy habit with blue-grey leaves, and the small pink flowers are borne in clusters at the end of the branches. 'Warley Ruber' makes a plant about 15cm/6in tall.

Removal of the flowering stems is not only a neat practice but assists with the propagation of the plant, as the non-flowering soft growth thus created is ideal for taking cuttings from midsummer onwards. Insert in a sand frame and pot up as soon as roots form. When established they should be pinched out and they will then be ready for planting out in the spring.

Take care
Do not plant in an acid soil.

Arabis ferdinandi-coburgi 'Variegata'
(Rock cress)
- **Full or partial sunshine**
- **Any soil**
- **Evergreen**

This evergreen perennial *A. ferdinandi-coburgi* 'Variegata' has conspicuous variegated foliage. It forms a tight mat up to 30cm/1ft across that is so attractive as to warrant the removal of the short white flowers borne on 8cm/3.2in stems. Unlike some plants, it retains its bright variegation throughout the year, which is a good reason to include it somewhere in the planting scheme.

Propagation is by division at almost any time, but it is best carried out during the late autumn or during early spring. Alternatively, cuttings can be taken with a heel, or some old wood at the base, in late summer.

This relative of the cabbage sometimes suffers from the same pests and diseases.

Take care
To retain the best variegation, do not give this plant too rich a diet.

Above: **Aethionema 'Warley Ruber'**
This hardy plant makes a brilliant display in the early summer months but needs to be kept going by cuttings each year.

Right: **Arenaria balearica**
This may be a difficult plant to establish but once it is settled into position it will spread gently to cover rock faces. Grow in shade.

Left: **Arabis ferdinandi-coburgi 'Variegata'**
Retaining its bright variegation throughout the year, the attractive foliage warrants the removal of the plant's short white flowers.

Arenaria balearica
(Corsican sandwort, Sandwort)
● **Moist shady situation**
● **Peaty soil**
● **Evergreen**

A quietly attractive plant that forms a prostrate mat of tiny green leaves, with masses of single white flowers on 2-3cm/0.8-1.25in stems. It requires a damp situation and will grow attractively over the face of a damp porous rock or peat block. I have found it difficult to establish, but once it does settle, it will stay. It is an unobtrusive plant, easy to eradicate if it becomes invasive, and although it spreads, it does so gently and with no harm to the plants it overruns. It comes from the Balearics and other Mediterranean islands; it can be seen in complete shade between rocks at sea level in Sardinia.

Propagation is by division in early autumn, planting direct. It dislikes being potted up, but this can be overcome by plunging a plant in peat and taking the pieces as they root.

Take care
This plant does not take kindly to direct exposure to sunshine.

Arisarum proboscideum
(Mousetail plant)
- Shady situation
- Leafy soil
- Deciduous

This is a curious little plant for a shady site in the peat garden or any shaded aspect, where it will spread inoffensively. It is of great attraction to children, as the 8-10cm/3.2-4in 'tails' at the end of the flower look like so many mice disappearing into the forest of arrow-shaped leaves. Dismissed by some people as a mere curiosity, this plant is not one of nature's most brightly coloured products, but its quiet charm is attractive to the discerning gardener.

The flower, which appears in spring, is technically a spathe, which is inflated and terminates in the 'tail'. It is olive green above and white beneath, with occasional purple striping. It is a native of central Italy and southern Spain.

Propagation is simply by division in late spring, after flowering; pot up in a peaty or leaf-mould compost. The leaves tend to die down or turn brown in late summer, so it should not be thought that the plant is dying.

Take care
This plant does not like full sun.

Astilbe chinensis 'Pumila'
(False goat's beard, Perennial spiraea)
- Moist shady situation
- Leafy soil
- Herbaceous

The mention of *Astilbe* may conjure up visions of the 1m/39in tall spikes of pink and dark red flowers found growing in wet spots by the side of ponds and streams in spring. The dwarf species are no less attractive, and are extremely useful for filling in the gap between spring and autumn, for they flower in the summer through to the early part of the autumn.

A. chinensis 'Pumila' produces a 23cm/9in tall narrow spike of deep pink flowers, slightly flushed with purple, from a base of fern-like leaves. It requires a cool spot, perhaps at the base of a rock where its roots can shelter. Full sun can be tolerated provided there is ample water in summer.

Propagation is by division in spring, taking care not to split the plants into too small units. The new young plants will certainly need moisture and a shady position while establishing, and should do well in a leafy or peaty soil.

Take care
Never let this plant dry out.

Left: **Arisarum proboscideum**
Suitable for any shaded position, this plant has distinctive flowers which appear in the spring. Do not plant in full sun.

Above: **Azorella trifurcata**
Sometimes catalogued under 'Bolax', this plant has a confused history, but it forms a neat and attractive cushion.

Azorella trifurcata

(Bolax glebaria)
- **Open situation but not direct sunshine**
- **Good drainage but with moisture**
- **Evergreen**

This is a rather confused plant, which has suffered from a name change and so may be found as *Bolax glebaria*. What is not in doubt is its habitat in South America, where it is native to the Falkland Islands and Chile.

It forms a spreading symmetrical mat on a stony sunny scree, which should have a degree of moisture about, or it can usefully be employed in the alpine house. The hummocks are composed of rosettes of leathery green leaves, and might make a spread of up to 90cm/3ft, but be only 7-8cm/2.75-3.2in tall. The flowers are minute and yellow, appearing in midsummer on short stems. The main claim to fame for this plant is its neat symmetry.

It spreads slowly, and this provides the method of propagation, as the spreading stems root as they go. Remove some rosettes in spring for propagation, and for neatness.

Take care
Do not expect a brilliant floral display from this particular plant.

Above: **Astilbe chinensis 'Pumila'**
Most astilbes like to grow beside water, but this dwarf form tolerates drier conditions and readily produces its pink spikes in late summer.

Campanula cochlearifolia
(C. pusilla)
(Fairies' thimbles)
● **Any situation**
● **Any soil**
● **Evergreen**

To choose just two examples from this huge
genus is an unkindness, when there are so many
that are such garden-worthy plants. However, *C.
cochlearifolia* (sometimes still listed as *C. pusilla*)
is so good-tempered as to be suitable for most
soils and situations. It is native to the European
Alps, where it thrives on and around limestone
rocks and is happiest in stony ground where it
can run freely. Thus in cultivation it enjoys scree
conditions where its blue bells can push their
way up on 5-8cm/2-3.2in stems from the heart-
shaped basal leaves. Although it spreads it can
be controlled very easily, but it is attractive
enough to deter such a move. There are forms
ranging from white to deep blue.

Propagation is by division between early
autumn and spring, or by soft cuttings in late
spring or early autumn.

Take care
This is not invasive, but give it space to roam.

Campanula poscharskyana
● **Sunny situation**
● **Not too rich a soil**
● **Evergreen**

This species has been described as
'rampageous but lovely', which conveys the
necessary warning for this attractive invader. The
plant forms a tangled mat of roots and stems that
is difficult to eradicate. Thus it is best planted
where it can be confined or in a corner where
nothing else will do well. It is ideal for a dry wall
or an area of poor soil, where it will produce
dozens of its clear lavender-blue bell-shaped
flowers on stems which are 30cm/1ft in height.
These flowers totally obscure the sharply-toothed
rounded leaves. The spread of a single plant can
be as much as 60-90cm/2-3ft.

An allied plant, only one degree less invasive,
is *C. portenschlagiana*, which has the additional
advantage of flowering well in shady situations.
Propagation is obviously no problem. Divide the
plant, probably with a spade, during the autumn
or in the spring.

Take care
Make sure that this attractive plant is starved,
and not planted near more precious subjects.

Above: **Campanula cochlearifolia**
*These flowers are a delight when seen in the
wild, and look equally attractive in cultivation. It is
happiest in stony ground.*

Corydalis cheilanthifolia
● **Prefers some sunshine**
● **Any soil**
● **Herbaceous**

The most desirable of this genus is the blue *Corydalis cashmiriana* from Kashmir, but it is not freely available, partly because of its fickle behaviour in dying out for no apparent reason. So we have to make do with *C. cheilanthifolia* from China, with ferny leaves and bright yellow flowers. It is a worthwhile plant, surviving well and seeding about unobtrusively in almost any soil. It tolerates more sun than most of the species, and the foliage takes on a bronzy hue when it has plenty of light. The flower spikes make the plant about 20cm/8in tall.

Propagation is by seed sown in late winter, or by seeking out self-sown seedlings in the garden. It is essential to sow seed thinly and to handle the seedlings before the main tap-root is formed. Young plants do not like staying in a pot for too long.

Take care
Put this plant in a place where there is plenty of room for it to seed about.

Above: **Campanula poscharskyana**
Suitable for growing in poor soil or up against a dry wall, this species is notoriously invasive and, once established, difficult to eradicate.

Below: **Corydalis cheilanthifolia**
A useful plant for every garden as it will grow in any soil and seeds almost unobtrusively. It will tolerate some sunshine.

Cyclamen hederifolium
(Alpine violet, Persian violet, Sowbread)
● Shade
● Soil with added leaf-mould
● Plant just under the surface

This Mediterranean cormous plant is hardy and will grow in poor soil, but it thrives if covered with a 2.5cm/1in layer of leaf-mould in late spring, after the leaves have died down. The plant grows to only 10cm/4in, often much less. The silvery leaves have dark green markings on the upper surface, and underneath they are red.

Plant the corms 10-15cm/4-6in apart in a light soil that is rich in leaf-mould. Grow cyclamen from seed: sow in pots or trays in late summer and leave the container outside on its side to prevent it becoming waterlogged. Germination will occur the following spring, and seedlings can be potted on, planting out when they are large enough to handle easily, in either late spring or late summer. Treat with a pesticide; disease is mainly due to wet conditions, so also treat the area with a fungicide.

Take care
Protect the corms from mice by covering with wire netting.

Dianthus neglectus
● Open situation
● Lime-free soil
● Evergreen

Pinks usually thrive on alkaline soils, but this is an exception, as it is to be found on lime-free soils in the eastern and southern European Alps. It forms a neat hummock of grey-green linear leaves that varies in height from 10-20cm/4-8in. It must be admitted that the flowers are variable, and so a good form must be chosen; the flowers are from pale pink to deep crimson, but always with a distinctive buff reverse. At best they are 3cm/1.25in across, on short stems that hold them just above the foliage, in midsummer.

This species does well in a sunny spot in well-drained soil, but it is important to note that it appreciates being moist in summer and less so in winter.

Propagation is by soft cuttings taken in midsummer from non-flowering shoots and inserted in a sandy cutting frame. The plants will be ready by late winter.

Take care
Do not plant in chalky or alkaline conditions as the plant will not thrive.

Below: **Cyclamen hederifolium**
This plant produces its flowers during late summer, which is a useful time of year to have colour on the rock garden. It is very easily raised from seed.

Diascia cordata

- **Warm open situation**
- **Well-drained soil**
- **Evergreen**

Plants from South Africa are usually suspect for hardiness, but this plant has seemed hardy now for some years. Perhaps its habitat at 2,500m/8,200ft in the Drakensberg Mountains has built up its resistance to winter cold. It is an attractive plant, producing 15-25cm/6-10in long racemes of pinky-terracotta flowers, 1.5cm/0.6in wide, from a dense mat of leafy stems.

It relishes a warm position in any well-drained soil, where it will flower in summer. Propagation is by cuttings of young shoots taken in summer and placed in a sand frame. When rooted these should be over-wintered in a frame before planting out the following spring.

Take care
Make sure this plant is not placed in an exposed situation.

Above: **Dianthus neglectus**
One of the gems of the large family of pinks which all thrive on alkaline soils and give such good displays in early summer.

Below: **Diascia cordata**
The terracotta-pink flowers come during summer. This plant definitely requires a warm situation that is not too exposed.

Epimedium alpinum

(Barrenwort)
- Shady corner
- Any soil
- Semi-evergreen

A widely distributed genus from the north temperate regions of Europe and Asia, including Japan. They are especially useful for ground cover in a semi-woodland or particularly shaded situation. The newly produced leaves in spring are an attractive fresh green, and colour nicely towards the autumn. *E. alpinum*, from the woodlands of Europe, has slightly toothed leaves, turning colour at the edges; it produces attractive racemes of flowers, the outer petals of which are pinky-red and the inner bright yellow.

Theoretically the plant is herbaceous, but the old leaves hang on over winter; they should be removed in spring to reveal the flowers before the new leaves grow up to hide them.

Propagation is by division in spring or autumn and potting into a leafy soil. Keep the pots in shade and the young plants will be ready for planting out in four to eight weeks.

Take care
Never let the soil dry out.

Above: **Epimedium alpinum**
This is a useful foliage plant for ground cover with unusual flowers that are hidden by the leaves. It will grow in a shady corner.

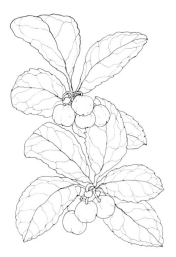

Above: **Euryops acraeus**
This dwarf shrub from South Africa has proven hardy in cultivation. The golden daisy-like flowers appear in summer.

Below: **Gaultheria procumbens**
A mildly vigorous carpet plant, this produces gorgeous scarlet berries and richly coloured foliage in the autumn.

Euryops acraeus
- Sunny situation
- Well-drained soil
- Evergreen shrub

This evergreen shrub from South Africa is remarkably hardy in the rock garden. It forms an upright bush, 30cm/1ft high, with bright silver leaves; the pure gold daisy flowers appear on short grey stems in summer.

It was originally thought to be tender, and confined to the alpine house, but it has proved better out of doors by making a neater shaped plant than when under glass. Over the years it forms a compact grey bush when given an open sunny position in a sharply drained soil.

Propagation is by cuttings of non-flowering shoots taken in summer and inserted in a sandy frame. However, there is usually a plentiful supply of suckers around the base of the plant, which can be removed with roots attached and potted up. Although the flowers are attractive, this is a plant grown mainly for its grey foliage.

Take care
Avoid damp situations, and prune the young shrub to a good shape.

Gaultheria procumbens
(Checkerberry, Mountain tea, Partridge berry, Wintergreen)
- Partial sunshine
- Leafy lime-free soil
- Evergreen ground cover

This hardy prostrate sub-shrub from America forms a mat of shiny dark evergreen oval leaves, 2.5cm/1in long and slightly toothed, which can spread to 1m/39in or more. Small white or pinkish bell-shaped flowers, about 5-6mm/0.19-0.23in long, appear at the tips of the shoots in late summer, followed by attractive bright red berries in autumn. The whole plant is no taller than 15cm/6in; it spreads by means of underground stems, and could be termed invasive, although it is easy to control.

G. procumbens is happier in a position with some but not total sunshine. It appreciates a cool moist leafy soil that is never allowed to dry out.

Propagation is by cuttings taken in early summer and inserted in the peat and sand frame, where they root easily. Pot up into peaty soil during the summer, and over-winter in a frame before planting in spring.

Take care
Allow room to spread.

Gentiana acaulis

(Stemless gentian)

- **Sunny but moist situation**
- **Prefers heavy soils**
- **Evergreen**

Of all the botanical names that are suspect, this is the classic. For years the experts have decreed this to be an invalid name, but everyone continues to use it, and we all know what is meant by *Gentiana acaulis* – the large blue trumpets on the grassy slopes of the Alps.

In gardens, however, they evoke a degree of frustration: either they will flower or they will not, for no apparent reason. They are happiest in a heavy loam and planted firmly. In desperation it has been suggested that they need to be trodden upon deliberately to encourage them to flower, as this emulates the treatment given them by cows in their native habitat. The 5-7.5cm/2-3in long trumpets appear above mid-green ovate leaves that can form a mat 45cm/18in across.

Propagation is by division in midsummer, potting into a good loam on the heavy side.

Take care
Move the plant about to encourage flowering.

Above right: **Gentiana acaulis**
The trumpet gentian of the Alps is of the deepest shades of blue, but it is rather temperamental in cultivation, sometimes failing to produce its blue trumpets.

Right: **Gentiana sino-ornata**
One of the delights of the autumn is to see a bed of these in flower. They prefer a cool site, with plenty of leaf-mould.

Gentiana sino-ornata
- Semi-shaded situation
- Acid soil
- Herbaceous

Of all the marvellous blue gentians, this is my favourite, coming at a time of the year when everything else is disappearing. To see a drift of this plant in autumn is an outstanding memory.

To achieve good results the plants should be divided every two or three years; this is easily done in spring, just as growth is beginning, by separating the thongs and replanting in a lime-free leafy soil. It is well worth the time and effort involved to obtain the best results from this plant, which will reward you with a mass of upturned brilliant blue 5cm/2in trumpets striped with deeper blue and green-yellow. Several named colour variants are good value, and there is an excellent white form.

Propagation is by division in spring, as mentioned, planting straight out into leafy soil.

Take care
Divide this plant regularly.

Above: **Iris cristata**
A dwarf iris from the southern USA that requires filtered sunlight to give of its best, so it could be well accommodated on the peat bed.

Iris cristata
- Likes semi-shade
- Grows in a neutral soil
- Herbaceous

It is extremely difficult to suggest a representative cross-section of this genus, which offers so much to rock gardens. The most easily obtained *I. reticulata* forms are so well known as not to need space here. The yellow *I. danfordiae* is also an excellent early spring bulb.

I. cristata has been described as one of the best of all the dwarf irises. The rhizome produces a fan of leaves up to 15cm/6in long, from which arise one or two flowers about 3-4cm/1.25-1.6in in diameter; these vary from lilac to purple or violet, but the form in general circulation is lilac-blue. It is a native of moist woods in eastern parts of North America, and therefore prefers peat soil and good drainage.

Propagation forms part of the cultivation routine for this plant, which should be lifted, divided and replanted from time to time, because it tends to die in the centre. Do this after flowering.

Take care
Never put this plant on a dry site.

Iris douglasiana

● Tolerates sunshine or shade
● Accepts any soil condition
● Evergreen

This is a very tough and free-flowering iris from the Pacific coast of North America; unfortunately, it is also very variable. It is 15-70cm/6-28in tall and the leaves are up to 2cm/0.8in wide. The branched stems have flowers which are 7-10cm/2.75-4in in diameter, and these vary from lavender to purple, with darker veins and a yellowish spot on the falls (outer petals); these appear in early summer. This plant benefits from a cool site in the rock garden, as its native habitat is in fields and light woodland.

Propagate with seed saved from the best forms, and sow in the autumn or spring in a temperature of 7-10°C/45-50°F in a seed compost. Plant the seedlings in spring when they are quite small, as the rhizomes resent disturbance when they become more mature; they will flower the following year. To maintain a good form, detach a young rhizome in the autumn and replant.

Take care
Never let young plants dry out.

Above: **Iris douglasiana**
An easy and vigorous plant that will do well in any soil, either light or heavy, and is not fussy about sunshine or shade.

Below: **Lavandula stoechas**
A native of the warmer climes of the Mediterranean, this lavender has proved to be more hardy than one would expect.

Above: **Linnaea borealis**
Forming a mat up to 60cm/2ft wide, this hardy plant produces delicate bell-shaped flowers in pairs. Prefers a shady position.

Lavandula stoechas
(French lavender, Spanish lavender)
● **Sunny situation**
● **Warm and light soil**
● **Almost hardy shrublet**

Common lavender is far too large for any rock garden, but its miniature cousin from the Mediterranean region – which forms a small bush up to 30cm/1ft tall in gardens, although taller in the wild – is a most suitable subject. Its slightly curious four-angled spikes of deep purple flowers, topped by a tuft of ovate purple bracts that persist after the plant has faded, appear in summer. It has the normal grey-green leaves of lavender.

Coming from the Mediterranean area, it does possess a degree of tenderness, but this can be overcome by keeping a supply of young plants. Either sow the seed during the winter in a seed compost, or take cuttings of non-flowering shoots during the early autumn and over-winter them in a frame.

Take care
It is particularly important to ensure that this plant has a sunny and well-drained corner of the garden to itself.

Linnaea borealis
(Twin-flower)
● **Shady position**
● **Leafy or peaty soil**
● **Ground cover**

The generic name of this plant commemorates the celebrated Carl von Linné (Linnaeus), the Swedish botanist. It is a plant that can be found in the colder regions of the northern hemisphere, which testifies to its hardiness. Forming a mat, it sends its wiry stems hither and thither in a tangle, from which emerge several delicate pink bell-shaped flowers in pairs on 5cm/2in stems. In ideal conditions, such as a cool aspect in shade or a north-facing peat bed, L. borealis will make a mat up to 60cm/2ft wide. There is also a slightly larger American form.

Propagation is tricky: it is necessary to grow a young plant on fast in a pan of sandy leaf-mould, which should be kept well watered from spring to autumn, and less so in winter. The runners should be pinned down to encourage rooting and then removed the following spring, ready for potting up and planting out in the autumn.

Take care
This is not a plant for full sunshine.

Oxalis adenophylla
- Full sun
- Sandy peaty soil
- Plant 5cm/2in deep

These 7.5cm/3in tall bulbous plants are ideal for the rock garden and edges of borders. They have delicate cup-shaped lilac-pink flowers 2.5cm/1in wide in midsummer, and small clusters of leaves that die down in winter.

The bulb-like rhizome should be planted in spring or autumn in a soil that is sandy but enriched with peat, leaf-mould or compost. Plant it 5cm/2in deep in a sunny place, although it will stand partial shade. Keep the plant moist during drought. When the bulbs have finished flowering in summer, they can be lifted, divided and replanted with more space around them. This can also be grown as a decorative pot plant, using a 20-25cm/8-10in pot and ordinary potting mixture. Keep it in the cool until ready to flower, and then bring it indoors. Every alternate year move it to a larger pot with fresh soil, or divide it and keep it in the same size pot with new potting mixture.

Take care
Label this plant, as its foliage dies down early in the season.

Penstemon newberryi
- Dry and sunny site
- Any soil
- Semi-evergreen

This plant is sometimes confused with *P. menziesii*, which it resembles. This is another genus where there is considerable confusion over the correct nomenclature. There are a number of attractive species, whatever their correct names may be, mostly originating in North America. Though technically hardy, they do suffer in severe winters, so a stock of young plants should be kept in reserve to cover any losses thus incurred. They do well in any open, well-drained soil, but an excess of moisture may kill them, so care is needed.

P. newberryi will form a bushy sub-shrub some 20cm/8in tall and will spread to 30-40cm/12-16in. Racemes of snapdragon-like pink to rose-purple flowers, about 3-4cm/1.25-1.6in long, appear in midsummer.

Propagation is by 5-7.5cm/2-3in long cuttings, taken in late summer or early autumn, which will be ready by the next spring. Seed, sown in winter, is variable.

Take care
Avoid wet conditions.

Phlox subulata 'McDaniel's Cushion'
(Moss phlox, Moss pink)
- Open sunny situation
- Neutral soil
- Evergreen

The true species of this technically sub-shrubby plant is never seen in cultivation, having been supplanted by several named varieties, lists of which can be found in specialist catalogues. 'Apple Blossom' is pale pink; 'G. F.' Wilson', clear lilac; and 'Temiscaming', a brilliant magenta-red. These form spreading mats up to 45cm/18in across and no more than 10cm/4in tall when in flower; they look particularly well cascading over rocks and dry walls, producing their 1.5-2cm/0.6-0.8in wide flowers *en masse* in late spring.

'McDaniel's Cushion', however, has a less spreading tendency, possibly a maximum of 25-30cm/10-12in at most, and so is suitable for the scree or where it cannot be overshadowed by taller plants.

Propagation is by soft cuttings taken in mid- to late summer and inserted in a sand frame.

Take care
Do not put more vigorous subjects near this variety.

Left: Oxalis adenophylla
Some oxalis are straightforward weeds and should be avoided. However, O. adenophylla is bulbous and well-behaved and enjoys being planted in full sunshine.

Above: **Penstemon newberryi**
There are numerous penstemons from
northwest America, ranging from pink to blue.
This one forms a shrub with pink flowers.

Below: **Phlox 'McDaniel's Cushion'**
This is one of the P. subulata cultivars that is
less spreading than its close relatives. It will
flower during the spring.

Polygala chamaebuxus
(Ground box, Milkwort)
- Light shade
- Peaty or leafy soil
- Evergreen sub-shrub

This spreading, ground-hugging shrub from the Alps does well in gardens. It forms small bushes 10-15cm/4-6in tall with box-like leaves and a spread of about 20-38cm/8-12in. Cream and yellow flowers tipped with purple appear from late spring to midsummer, up to six flowers on each stem. In the form illustrated, the flowers are carmine and yellow, and thus slightly more spectacular. This may be seen catalogued as 'Purpurea', 'Rhodoptera' or 'Grandiflora'. Growing as it does on the edge of woodland, this species appreciates a leafy soil and some light shade where possible.

Propagation is by soft cuttings taken in mid- to late summer and inserted in the shaded peat frame. Pot on, making sure to pinch out the tips to obtain a bushy plant. The plants can be divided in spring.

Take care
Not a plant for a hot sunny corner.

Potentilla crantzii
(Cinquefoil)
- Sunny exposure
- Any soil
- Herbaceous

An inhabitant of grassy meadows in the Alps, North America and Asia, this species is both useful and hardy. It forms a tuft of 5-15cm/2-6in stalks, with small palmate leaves and broad-petalled yellow flowers blotched orange at the base of each of the petals.

The flowering period in gardens is mid- to late summer, and the length of the flowering stem depends on the plant's environment and whether it is drawn up by its neighbours. It does well on a light open soil and in full sun, where it will flower superbly. In its native habitat it lives in a limey soil, but in cultivation it is quite accommodating in this respect.

There are two ways of propagating this plant: by seed, in late winter or early spring, though this may not result in the right plant; and by division in the autumn, which is preferable.

Take care
Do not let this plant be overshadowed.

Below: **Polygala chamaebuxus 'Rhodoptera'**
This colourful subject is a small shrubby plant which will thrive in the peat garden. It needs light shade to give of its best.

Above: **Potentilla crantzii**
A sun-loving and summer-flowering plant from the Arctic areas of Europe, Asia and America; its yellow flowers have a basal orange blotch.

Primula frondosa
- Semi-shade
- Peaty soil
- Herbaceous

A neat, pretty little plant that forms a rosette of attractive grey-green leaves with farina (mealy coating) on the undersides. Flower stems up to 15cm/6in bear masses of pink-lilac to red-purple 1cm/0.4in wide miniature primrose flowers, sometimes with a white eye.

P. frondosa is found near melting snow by shady cliffs in the Balkans, and so in cultivation prefers a moist, peaty soil, lightly shaded. It thrives in a west- or east-facing peat bed or in the lee of a rock away from direct sunshine.

Propagation is by seed sown in late summer or late winter. Fresh seed is best, as in all the primrose family; pot up in the spring, and plant in early autumn.

Take care
Although it likes a moist site, this plant does not like it too damp.

Above: **Primula frondosa**
A rosette-forming species with grey-green leaves, it produces rose-lilac flowers in spring. It thrives in any lightly shaded moist position.

107

Ranunculus gramineus
- Sun or partial shade
- Any soil
- Herbaceous

This herbaceous perennial is a member of the buttercup family and an extremely valuable plant to have in the garden. Buttercup flowers are produced in sprays on 30cm/1ft stems. The leaves are grey-green and grass-like. Appearing from late spring to midsummer, the yellow blooms are 2cm/0.8in in diameter, shiny in texture and very free flowering. Mainly used in drifts in slightly moist areas, these plants will also give a good account of themselves in most borders and beds.

Raise plants each year from seed by sowing in a frame or under cloches. Sow directly into the ground during early spring in shallow drills. Thin out the seedlings and remove the frame top or cloche in mid-spring. Grow on until the autumn, then plant them out in their final flowering positions. Keep young plants cool through the summer months.

Take care
Does not need a wet situation.

Roscoea cautleoides
- Light shade
- Cool soil
- Herbaceous

It has been said that roscoeas hardly qualify as alpine plants, but by common usage on rock gardens they merit inclusion in this list. Of them all, *R. cautleoides* is probably the most handsome. Its mid-green lanceolate leaves reach from 30-40cm/12-16in and a profusion of soft luminous yellow orchid-like flowers appear just above this foliage in summer.

They prefer a cool situation, the peat garden being an appropriate spot where they can enjoy the moist peaty soil.

Propagation is by division of the dormant roots in spring. Self-sown seedlings can be potted up in late summer, or seed sown in late winter, keeping the young plants shaded during the summer. The roots do not like being confined in a small pot, so ensure that you do not delay planting out.

Take care
Plant roscoeas deeply and they will survive hard winters.

Left: **Ranunculus gramineus**
This buttercup with grass-like leaves produces its cup-shaped flowers on tallish stems during the late spring. Grow in sun or semi-shade.

Above: **Saponaria ocymoides**
The soapwort is happy to cascade over a stone wall or rocks, where the mass of pink flowers can be seen to best advantage.

Saponaria ocymoides
(Soapwort)
● **Open sunny situation**
● **Well-drained soil**
● **Evergreen**

An invaluable plant for every rock garden or rock wall, where its prostrate mat looks well cascading down over the rocks. It is a plant of shingle banks in the Alps of south-western and south central Europe, which indicates its need for good drainage. The mats can be 30cm/1ft across and are covered with 1cm/0.4in wide pink flowers that appear from mid- to late summer.

There are two selected forms: 'Compacta', which is slower-growing and less vigorous; and 'Rubra Compacta', with rich carmine flowers. They are all easy to cultivate.

Propagation is very easy by soft cuttings in summer, taken from non-flowering wood and placed in a sand frame. It is necessary to stop the young plants at least twice to get a tidy young plant.

Take care
Give this plant room to expand.

Above: **Roscoea cautleoides**
This less common plant has unusual flowers that thrive in the moist cool conditions of the peat bed. Summer-flowering, it needs light shade.

Saxifraga cochlearis

- Open sunny position
- Well-drained limestone scree
- Evergreen

The encrusted saxifrages form rosettes of grey-green leaves that are often attractively encrusted with spots of lime around the edges. *S. cochlearis* is found on limestone rocks in the Maritime Alps, which gives a lead to its requirements in cultivation: a well-drained situation, ideally on scree.

The form 'Minor' is ideal for planting in a trough, and forms an extremely neat hummock of grey-leaved rosettes, from which shoot sprays of 1.5cm/0.6in wide milk-white flowers in early summer, no taller than 10cm/4in. Propagation is by detaching the side rosettes in late summer, preferably with some roots attached, and potting them on into a lime soil; or they can be planted out direct.

Take care
This plant needs good drainage and a lime soil.

Tropaeolum polyphyllum

- Sunny position
- Deep and well-drained soil
- Herbaceous

This is a spectacular species that seems difficult to establish, but it is worth the effort, as it is so distinctive and showy. It is a tuberous-rooted perennial, which sends up long trailing or arching stems of grey leaves, in the axils of which are produced large rich yellow nasturtium-like flowers in early and mid-summer. It dies away after flowering and is likely to come up in a completely different spot the following year.

The secret of success is to plant the tuber at least 30cm/1ft deep, in a position where its trailing stems can hang down over a rock or wall. Its hardiness has long been proven.
Once the plant is established, propagation is simple, by digging up the tubers as required.

Take care
Plant deep, and allow space for this desirable plant to spread.

Above: **Tropaeolum polyphyllum**
This spectacular species from Chile produces long stems clothed in grey leaves, with masses of yellow flowers appearing in midsummer.

Right: **Saxifraga cochlearis 'Minor'**
The photograph shows only the flower of this encrusted saxifrage; its silver-edged rosettes form a tight clump. It is happy growing in tufa and is most appropriate for a trough.

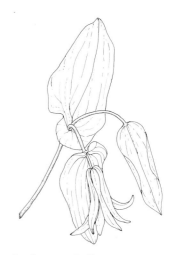

Uvularia perfoliata
(Strawbell, Throatwort)
● **Light shade**
● **Leafy soil**
● **Herbaceous**

This small genus of hardy plants, from the woods of North America, is related to the lily, and has a rhizomatous root system. They are ideal for a shady part of the rock or peat garden. A single upright stem, about 20-25cm/8-10in tall, appears in late spring, with pointed heart-shaped leaves on the upper part. Numerous pendent pale yellow narrow bell-shaped flowers are found, singly or in pairs, at the tips of branchlets. The leaves are perfoliate, meaning that the main stem appears to pass through them.

The best time for propagation is in summer when the plants can be divided and potted up in leafy soil and kept moist and shaded. Division in mid-autumn is possible but brings the possibility of greater loss in winter.

Take care
This is not a plant for the sunny rock garden; it prefers some shade.

Left: **Uvularia perfoliata**
This relation of the lily spreads by underground rhizomes. It prefers a cool corner and is happy on the peat bed, where it should be marked well because the foliage dies down early in the growing season.

111

Index of Common Names